SPARKLING

SPARKLING

Champagne and Sparkling Cocktails for Any Occasion

ELVA RAMIREZ

UNION
SQUARE
& CO.

NEW YORK

UNION SQUARE & CO. and the distinctive Union Square & Co. logo
are trademarks of Sterling Publishing Co., Inc.

Union Square & Co., LLC, is a subsidiary of Sterling Publishing Co., Inc.

Text © 2024 Elva Ramirez
Photographs © 2024 Robert Bredvad

ISBN 978-1-4549-5377-7
ISBN 978-1-4549-5378-4 (e-book)

For information about custom editions, special sales, and premium purchases,
please contact specialsales@unionsquareandco.com.

Printed in China

2 4 6 8 10 9 7 5 3 1

unionsquareandco.com

Editor: Caitlin Leffel
Designer: Renée Bollier
Food Stylist: Mallory Lance
Prop Stylist: Maeve Sheridan
Project Editor: Ivy McFadden
Production Manager: Kevin Iwano

To Will Davis, forever bestie.
Champagne for my real friends.

CONTENTS

INTRODUCTION

· ·

FOR CENTURIES, Champagne has been synonymous with celebration. Its hold on the popular imagination has never wavered.

While the Gauls were likely making wine before they were conquered by the Romans, winemaking in Reims, France, started in earnest in 282 CE following a Roman edict. Within a few generations, the still wines produced in Reims grew to such fame that kings, courtiers, and high clergy made a point of making visits to the area to taste the local product. By the Middle Ages, the French established a tradition of royal coronations at the magnificent Reims Cathedral, where "wine flowed in rivers." Even before its signature innovation, Rémois wine, given its prestigious presence at coronations, was already considered the "ordinary drink of kings and princes."

The innovations of one French monk in the late 1670s unlocked wine's potential. Dom Pérignon is credited as the greatest winemaker of his age, and perhaps in the history of winemaking, and his reputation was built on his talent for wine blending, or "marrying" multiple wines. While this is a common feature of Champagne today, it was revolutionary at the time. The monk was also the first to make clear white wine out of black grapes; before then, the wine was an unappetizing gray or pale straw color. Given that his blends featured multiple plots and varietals, the monk stamped his own name on his bottles, an early exercise in brand marketing. As Pérignon's reputation as a winemaker grew, "his name became identified with the wine of the abbey," Henry Vizetelly writes in an early Champagne history book. "People asked for the wine of Pérignon, til they forgot that he was a man and not a vineyard, and within a year of his death, his name figures amongst a list of the wine-producing slopes of the Champagne."

While today the name "Dom Pérignon" conjures images of luxurious bubbles, many experts point out that the monk spent many years fighting against the light fizz that occurred naturally following secondary fermentation in bottles. As historian Tilar Mazzeo notes, Pérignon was actually "given the task of finding a way to get rid of the bubbles ruining the local wines." Lightly fizzy wines had been a troublesome feature of Rémois wines dating back centuries, and before secondary fermentation was fully understood, the buildup of bubbles and variations in the thickness of bottles could result in exploding vintages.

Despite a popular misconception that Dom Pérignon "invented" carbonation in bottles, historians agree that the British first discovered how to alchemize still wine into bubbles. Wealthy British consumers who sought to protect their French wine from oxidation began storing their prized liquids in bottles instead of barrels. By sealing their wines and adding a dose of brandy as a preservative, the British found that their still wines took on a bit of sparkle, which they, unlike the French at the time, found quite desirable. "In their efforts to preserve imported still wines from the Champagne, [the British] had haphazardly started the process of secondary fermentation required to make sparkling Champagne," Mazzeo reports. The historian notes that the British were converting wine into Champagne by the 1670s, "a full decade before the wine was first produced in France."

The first Champagne house, Maison Ruinart, was founded in September 1729 by Nicolas Ruinart. The opportunity provided by a new wine category prompted plucky entrepreneurs and family businesses to join the fray. Considered the start-ups of their day, these Champagne brands are now recognizable as glittery maisons with names such as Clicquot, Krug, and Moët & Chandon. Their bet, which was far from a sure thing at the time, paid off handsomely.

By 1895, 80 percent of all the Champagne drunk in America was quaffed in a small section of New York City between Fifth and Eighth Avenues, and Twenty-Third and Thirty-Fourth Streets, the New York Journal reported. Over 200,000 barrels of Champagne were consumed that year in New York, notching over $5.3 million in sales in late-1890s dollars (equivalent to more than $181 million in 2023).

If that seems like a lot, that milestone was quickly surpassed just four years later, when the city beat its own Champagne-drinking record. Over 33 million quarts of Champagne were imported in 1899, with over half the entire haul consumed in New York. "This is the greatest Champagne year New York has ever known. The desire to 'celebrate' is the cause of it," the Journal reported in August 1899.

At the height of the Gilded Age, Champagne firmly lodged in the American consciousness as the ultimate luxury product; the move was reflected by high society taking on "Champagne" as a synonym for aspirational style and timeless elegance.

Fashion articles tracked the emergence of a color referred to as "champagne" as the "It" hue for gowns and dresses. The New York Tribune's fashion reporter predicted the end-of-year trends for 1900: "Two new colors which are reported as likely this winter are known as 'champagne' and 'champagne froth.' The first is decidedly pretty and is a delicate pinkish-amber shade. The second is almost white, but with the faintest possible touch of flesh-colored pink." In 1904, the Tribune waxed poetic over the new silks available for dressmaking at a store on Twenty-Third Street: "Take, for instance, a piece of champagne color, which reflects a tint like the heart of a topaz . . ."

The popularity of Champagne—the beverage, that is—in the late 1890s coincides with the start of another cultural moment: the birth of the cocktail era. The first cocktail recipe book, Jerry Thomas' Bar-Tenders Guide: How to Mix All Kinds of Plain and Fancy Drinks, was published in 1862. A seminal relic of the pre-Prohibition era, the book features recipes for classics such as juleps, Manhattans, and toddies. Thomas also included multiple recipes for Champagne-based cocktails and sparkling wine punches (one of which has been adapted for this book), illustrating that cocktails and Champagne have been intertwined since both were fairly new phenomena. Champagne appeared in the wave of influential cocktail books that followed, including *Cocktail Boothby's American Bartender* (1891) and *Stuart's Fancy Drinks and How to Mix Them* (1904). The charm of a well-made Champagne cocktail would inspire both a British prince and one of America's most famous authors, as well as countless mixologists, to design their own recipes.

Champagne isn't the only wine with bubbles, of course. The popularity of Champagne prompted other regions to craft their own sparkling blends. Effervescent wines from Spain, Italy, the United States, and others introduced different flavor profiles and new winemaking technology while also redefining occasions for drinking. Bubbly drinks are shorthand for "good times" everywhere from movie montages to song lyrics to wedding receptions.

Given our contemporary interest in mixology as well as the long history of the sparkling wine cocktail, it makes sense that the effervescent cocktail is overdue for a moment in the spotlight.

Sparkling is designed for how we drink now: More than just a special-occasions-only or once-a-year moment, bubbles are now recognized as the perfect companion for nearly every event, from casual solo dinners to festive brunch parties to late-night romantic rendezvous. As a Champagne expert once memorably told me, "You drink bubbles when the sky is blue."

The following collection of recipes includes famous classics as well as delightful originals from top bartenders. You'll find large-format recipes sure to be hits at your next party, as well as single servings that will imbue any moment with elegance.

Full of sumptuous drink recipes to elevate even a casual gathering, *Sparkling* reminds us that *every* moment is an opportunity to enjoy a glass of dancing bubbles fit for royalty.

MAKING SPARKLING COCKTAILS AT HOME

Before you start making drinks, here are a few things to keep in mind.

INVEST IN QUALITY BAR AND KITCHEN TOOLS

- Purchase tools and glassware from bartending or culinary brands, such as industry favorites Cocktail Kingdom or Food52. You'll need cocktail and culinary measuring tools, including a mixing glass, bar spoons, cocktail shakers, strainers, and proper jiggers. My go-to tool is Cocktail Kingdom's copper Japanese-style jigger, which has measurements from ½ ounce to 2 ounces.

- If you will be making large-format punches, you'll need pitchers (such as iced tea pitchers or drink dispensers) for serving. If the serving pitchers are too small to prepare the punch in, mix it in a large soup pot and then transfer smaller batches to decorative bottles or other serving containers.

- You'll also need ice molds in various sizes, including large molds if you plan on making large-format punches. You can improvise when making large ice for punches; I've used ice pop molds as well as medium-size storage containers to make big blocks of ice.

- A Breville juicer is a worthy investment and is the first step for making high-quality cocktails at home, given how many drinks rely on fresh-pressed juices.

- You'll need a variety of straining tools, from fine-mesh cocktail strainers to strainers that can sit on top of containers. Finely woven fabrics, such as linen napkins, muslin nut-milk bags, and coffee filters will be needed for straining syrups and other liquids.

- A variety of glass containers for storage and plastic containers for freezing are essential. I extend the life of my syrups by breaking up bigger batches into smaller portions and using only what I need. Many syrups can be used in multiple scenarios, from other cocktails to smoothies to coffee and tea drinks.

Be careful with using glass for freezing, as some bottles can break when the frozen liquid expands.

....

- Invest in several quality sparkling wine stoppers. Cuisinart and Kloveo offer durable versions that work as promised and don't fall apart easily. If you have wine left over, a proper stopper will keep it fresh for several days. The best stoppers create an airtight seal to prevent oxidation and maintain carbonation. Some of my best stoppers have extended a bottle's lifetime for a minimum of three days and sometimes up to a week.

....

- Most people have basic kitchen measuring spoons, cups, and glasses, but it's worth mentioning that these will be needed as well.

WINE AND SPIRITS OPTIONS

Which sparkling wine goes best in a cocktail? Suggestions are listed in recipes, but if your local wine store is out of a particular brand, here's a few things to keep in mind:

- You don't have to, nor should you, spend too much on wine that will be used in cocktails. Aged fine Champagnes (such as Dom Pérignon, Ruinart, Krug, Lallier, and others) have subtle flavors and will have smaller bubbles (as a result of their time spent in cellars), so a fine Champagne's best features will be lost in a cocktail, especially if it has fresh juice in it. (Though for sparkling cocktails with a minimum of ingredients, such as a Kir Royale, a fine wine is an excellent choice.)

....

- Look for young wines from a range of producers (American, Italian, British, Spanish, and French). Inexpensive, sparkling wines are produced via the charmat or Martinetti method (in which bubbles are formed in stainless steel vats before being transferred into bottles). Charmat wines tend to have fruity, fresh qualities and soft bubbles that dissipate quickly. Prosecco and Lambrusco are the most well-known examples of wines made via charmat.

....

- Sometimes, young wines can be acidic, which will work with (or against) a cocktail's palate; taste as you go and don't pour too much wine into a drink all at once, such that you undermine the work you just put into preparing it.

- All Champagne and some sparkling wines are produced using the *methodo classico* or the Champenoise style; a wine's second fermentation, which results in bubbles, occurs inside the bottle. Champenoise production requires time and aging in cellars, which is one reason these wines tend to be more expensive than their charmat peers. This traditional style typically translates into expressive wines with buttery, drier qualities and a stronger carbonation. While some traditional method wines can be more expensive than wines made via charmat, it's easy to find many affordable examples of traditional sparkling wines, including French sparklers, Spanish Cava, and wines from Italian producers in Trentino and Franciacorta.

- Which spirits or liqueurs can be replaced? It depends. You don't have to buy a new bottle of tequila if you already have a blanco in the house. Base spirits such as gin, vodka, and rum allow for some interchangeability. Liqueurs, however, tend to be quite specific, with distinct profiles and colors; try to use the liqueur listed in the recipes as much as possible. That said, almost every liqueur has a rival with similar virtues that can be a last-minute stand-in if you can't find the original ingredient.

- Wine and spirits store employees know a lot and are often enthusiastic resources. Ask questions and take their recommendations.

INGREDIENTS CHOICE AND STORAGE

- Properly chilling all sparkling wines before use is essential.

- Juice should always be freshly pressed, not bottled. A rule of thumb: Bad fruit yields bad juice; if you wouldn't eat it, don't juice it.

- Citrus juice (especially lemon and lime) is volatile and has a window of 4 to 12 hours, after which it begins to denature, resulting in cloudiness and changes in flavor. As I note in several recipes, when preparing drinks for an event, you can combine all the alcoholic elements (except sparkling wine or sparkling water) first, and then add the freshly pressed juice in the last hour before guests arrive. This ensures the freshest possible taste.

- Use the best quality mixers, such as Fever-Tree and London Essence, which have less sugar and stronger bubbles than their peers. Supermarket tonics and seltzers may overwhelm delicate cocktail flavors.

  ....

- When making syrups, always strain away all the solids. Let syrups fully cool before covering and storing.

  ....

- Label and date containers. It seems obvious, but it's very easy to lose track of when something was made, especially if there are multiples.

  ....

- Wine-based liqueurs, such as vermouth, should be refrigerated after opening.

  ....

- Never use another cork to store an opened bottle of sparkling wine; the pressure can cause the cork to eject and can cause injury or damage to your kitchen.

  ....

- Kalustyan's in New York City is the bar world's source for everything from loose teas to hard-to-find bitters to fruit purees and other nonalcoholic ingredients. You can find them online at https://foodsofnations.com.

MAKING DRINKS

- Practice mise en place, which means setting up a clean space with all the products and tools neatly laid out before you start. This prevents unnecessary hunting and distractions.

  ....

- If you're nervous about spillage or wobbly hands when pouring liquids into a jigger, you may get more accurate measurements if you place the jigger on a flat surface (rather than holding it high like a star bartender who does this every day). Fill it up and then carefully pour the liquid into a mixing tin. As with any tool, it takes a little practice, but it's easy to get used to.

  ....

- Batch drinks like they do at world-class bars. Rather than making drinks individually, you can measure out ingredients and premix them so that when guests arrive, all you need to do is pour over ice and add a splash of wine, if needed. Batching drinks ahead of time will allow you to focus on hosting rather than bartending.

....

- Many, if not all, recipes in this collection have the sparkling wine added at the end. There's a few reasons for that. One: You should never shake a fizzy liquid (wine or soda) in a mixing tin. The pressure will cause the container to explode. Two: You don't want to bruise the delicate bubbles of the wine. Once you've added the wine, you can give the drink one last gentle stir to combine and then serve. You want to preserve the bubbly freshness that occurs when the wine is just added.

....

- If you have the space, chill glasses before serving.

....

- Unless the recipe says otherwise, always use fresh ice in a glass and toss the broken ice that's used in the mixing tin.

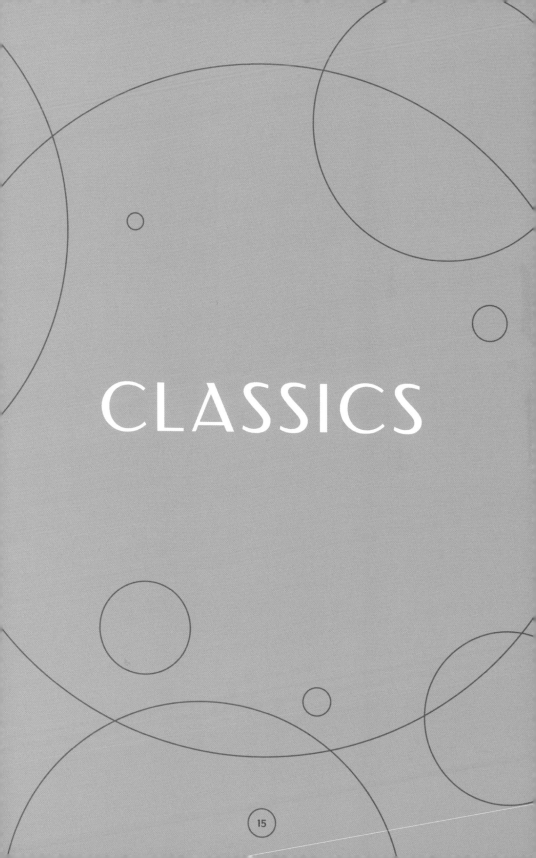

CLASSICS

APEROL SPRITZ

MAKES 1 DRINK

3 ounces chilled Prosecco, preferably Cinzano

2 ounces Aperol

1 ounce chilled soda water, to top

Orange slice, for garnish

This classic summertime drink really is as easy as "3, 2, 1." Three ingredients, in easy-to-remember proportions, combine to make the most recognizable ambassador in the spritz category. This bittersweet yet sprightly Aperol Spritz is an approachable introduction to the Italian aperitivo hour, which remains the most elegant way to pass the time between sun-drenched days and languid sunsets.

For the most authentic experience, use the fresh and fruity Cinzano Prosecco, which, like Aperol, is also produced by Campari Group and is recommended as its ideal pairing.

Pour the Prosecco and Aperol into a wine glass filled with ice. Stir gently to combine. Top with the soda water and garnish with the orange slice.

FRENCH 75

MAKES 1 DRINK

1 ounce gin, such as Sweet Gwendoline French gin

¼ ounce fresh lemon juice

¼ ounce simple syrup (see page 168)

2 ounces chilled Champagne, to top

Lemon twist, for garnish

Classic never goes out of style. Case in point: the French 75, one of the world's most famous Champagne cocktails. The drink dates to around the late 1920s and is named after a type of rapid-fire gun used by the French during World War I. The cocktail appears in Harry Craddock's seminal *Savoy Cocktail Book* (1930), in which the famed bartender sardonically notes that the drink "hits with remarkable precision."

This recipe lands on the drier side of the traditional iteration, with just a whisper of lemon juice and sugar. My version is more gin-forward, giving you an opportunity to see how different gins play out in the drink. Consider swapping in a new gin each time you make one. Some suggestions: Start with bartender favorites Fords gin and Hendricks gin, then move on to upstarts like Sweet Gwendoline and Citadelle, which are both French-style formulations.

In a mixing tin, combine the gin, lemon juice, and simple syrup. Fill with ice and shake well until very cold. Strain into a flute. Top with the Champagne and garnish with the lemon twist.

NEGRONI SBAGLIATO

MAKES 1 DRINK

1 ounce Campari

1 ounce sweet vermouth, preferably Cinzano 1757 Vermouth di Torino Rosso

1 ounce chilled Prosecco, preferably Cinzano

Orange slice, for garnish

The Negroni Sbagliato is a summertime classic that emerged out of *La Dolce Vita*–era Italy. According to Campari lore, the drink was born in 1968 when Milanese bartender Mirko Stocchetto mistakenly used Prosecco instead of gin when making a Negroni at Milan's historic Bar Basso. The "mistaken Negroni" remained a discreet cult favorite of cocktail fans until 2022, when a viral social media video with two actresses ("Negroni. Sbagliato . . . with Prosecco in it.") thrust the drink into the global spotlight.

For the most authentic experience, opt for this all-Italian recipe straight from Campari HQ, which features their preferred Prosecco, Cinzano.

In a rocks glass filled with ice, combine the Campari and vermouth. Stir to combine. Top with the Prosecco and quickly stir once more to incorporate. Garnish with the orange slice.

DEATH IN THE AFTERNOON

MAKES 1 DRINK

½ ounce absinthe

¼ ounce simple syrup
(see page 168)

Well-chilled Champagne
or sparkling wine, to top

This classic drink is the invention of Ernest Hemingway, and it first appears in the 1935 book *So Red the Nose*, a collection of cocktails by celebrity authors including Edgar Rice Burroughs and Theodore Dreiser. The book opens with Hemingway's missive to pour "one jigger of absinthe into a Champagne glass . . . until it attains the proper opalescent milkiness. Drink 3 to 5 of these slowly." The author apparently came up with the concoction alongside three naval officers of the HMS *Danae*. The book's editors, Sterling North and Carl Kroch, dryly note, "It takes a man with hair on his chest to drink five Absinthe and Champagne Cocktails and still handle the English language in the Hemingway fashion."

Whether you choose to heed Hemingway's instructions or not, this drink (adapted from the original to reduce the absinthe and add a touch of sugar) delivers a punch of flavor with a minimum of effort. It is slightly opaque as a result of the absinthe, which also provides a signature black licorice backdrop that isn't overwhelming. Feel free to punch up the absinthe to ¾ ounce, if black licorice is your thing.

In a wine glass, combine the absinthe and simple syrup. Stir once to combine. Top with Champagne.

ST-GERMAIN SPRITZ

MAKES 1 DRINK

1½ ounces St-Germain elderflower liqueur

2 ounces chilled sparkling wine, preferably Martini & Rossi Prosecco

2 ounces chilled soda water

Lemon twist, for garnish

Edible flowers, for garnish (optional)

The chic girl's drink of choice, the St-Germain Spritz is a cocktail version of the little black dress that never goes out of style. Perky and sparkly, this drink brings St-Germain's recognizable elderflower flavor to the foreground, while the wine and soda water provide a crisp, snappy finish. Between its low alcohol content and its elegant sweetness, this is a crowd-pleasing drink to serve all year long.

Pour the St-Germain into a tall glass filled with ice and stir quickly. Top with the sparkling wine and soda water. Gently express the lemon twist over the top of the glass, and garnish with edible flowers, if desired.

PRINCE OF WALES'S
COCKTAIL

MAKES 1 DRINK

1 teaspoon confectioners' sugar

1 dash Angostura bitters

1½ ounces rye whiskey

¼ teaspoon maraschino liqueur

1 small cube of pineapple (see Note)

Chilled Champagne, to top

1 lemon peel

NOTE

Wondrich notes that a fresh pineapple cube (about an inch or so long) is best, but a small wedge of canned pineapple can be used, provided it is not dripping in syrup.

Bartenders and cocktail enthusiasts everywhere owe a massive debt to historian David Wondrich, the foremost authority on how drinks evolved from their pre-Prohibition golden age to now. His meticulous research includes not just uncovering drink recipes that may have otherwise been lost to time, but updating them with contemporary specs (which is important, given how products and measuring tools have evolved over the past hundred years or so). In his James Beard Award–winning book *Imbibe!*, Wondrich unearths the Prince of Wales's cocktail, created by HRH Prince Albert Edward, the louche son of Queen Victoria. Given that his mother was one of the UK's longest-serving monarchs, the prince had little to do for most of his life but become something of a flaneur, resulting in his take on the Improved Whiskey Cocktail, which Wondrich calls "one of the sportiest on record." Had circumstances been different, Wondrich writes, "Albert Edward, Prince of Wales, would've made a hell of a bartender."

In a mixing tin, combine the sugar, bitters, and ½ teaspoon water. Stir until the sugar dissolves. Add the rye, maraschino liqueur, and pineapple, then shake briskly to break up the pineapple. Strain into a chilled coupe and top with Champagne. Express the oils from the lemon peel over the top of the glass, then discard.

KIR ROYALE

MAKES 1 DRINK

½ ounce crème de cassis liqueur

Well-chilled rosé Champagne, to top

Lemon twist, for garnish

The Kir Royale, one of the most famous Champagne cocktails, is credited to Canon Félix Kir, a French priest who was part of the French Resistance during World War II. The original Kir cocktail mixes black currant cordial with white wine. The Kir Royale (a "royale" is a drink that's been updated with wine bubbles) is a mix of black currant liqueur and Champagne. While the traditional Kir Royale features white wine, I prefer the saturated berry tones and fruity notes that a sparkling rosé teases out in both palate and color.

Pour the crème de cassis into a flute. Fill the glass with Champagne and gently stir once to combine. Garnish with the lemon twist.

PORN STAR MARTINI

MAKES 1 DRINK

1½ ounces vanilla vodka, preferably Grey Goose La Vanille or Absolut Vanilla

½ ounce Chinola passion fruit liqueur

2 ounces passion fruit puree, preferably Boiron

1 teaspoon vanilla sugar, preferably Oaktown Spice

Passion fruit slice, for garnish

2 ounces chilled Champagne

No Champagne cocktail collection is complete without a mention of the late Douglas Ankrah's lauded Porn Star Martini. Launched into the world at London's Townhouse in 2003, the cheekily named Porn Star Martini is a vehicle for a sinful coupling of passion fruit and vanilla, finished with a serving of luxurious chilled Champagne on the side (some might call it, er, a literal "money shot"). Ankrah, who passed away in August 2021, gifted bartending with a luscious sip that people will be enjoying for decades to come.

There are always questions about how to drink the Champagne shot. The crispness of the wine is functional. It acts as a palate cleanser that cuts through the drink's candied sweetness; the two palates play off each other, with each enhancing subtleties in the other. Feel free to alternate sips between the two, or save the wine for last. Ankrah was known to tell people to drink the shot however they wanted, even if that meant pouring the shot into the coupe.

In a mixing tin filled with ice, combine the vodka, Chinola, passion fruit puree, and vanilla sugar. Shake briskly to combine. Strain into a chilled martini glass or coupe and garnish with the passion fruit slice. Pour the Champagne into a shot glass and serve it on the side.

ORIGINALS

BISOUS BISOUS

MAKES 1 DRINK

1 ounce Cap Corse quinquina vermouth

½ ounce Suze herbal liqueur

¼ ounce Giffard Crème de Pêche de Vigne liqueur

3 dashes citric acid solution (see page 171)

Chilled Champagne, to top

After the Negroni Sbagliato went viral in 2022 (see page 21), bartenders everywhere were bombarded with orders for the classic Italian drink. At New York's Discolo, Marc du Jonchay's version, featuring all-French ingredients, stands apart from the crowd. In his cheeky riff, peach liqueur is set loose to play with Cap Corse, a French quinine vermouth, and Suze, a storied herbal liqueur, then capped with a crown of Champagne bubbles. The result: The cocktail equivalent of paying homage to an iconic classic yet finding something completely new to say at the same time.

In a rocks glass filled with ice, combine the vermouth, Suze, peach liqueur, and citric acid solution. Stir briskly to combine. Top with Champagne.

All wine-based spirits, including vermouth, should be refrigerated once opened to prevent oxidation.

CAUSEWAY CUP

MAKES 1 DRINK

1½ ounces Volcan de Mi Tierra X.A reposado tequila

1½ ounces pineapple juice

½ ounce Midori

½ ounce fresh lime juice

¼ ounce simple syrup (see page 168)

Chilled sparkling wine

Orange wheel, for garnish

Delicate and fragrant, Trevor Easton Langer's Causeway Cup unfurls a beguiling bouquet of citrus and melon, which is tempered by aged tequila. Perhaps the most luxurious drink in this collection, the sumptuously peridot cocktail features Volcan de Mi Tierra's X.A reposado, an ultra-premium spirit that's a heady blend of reposado, añejo, and extra añejo tequilas. The result is a nuanced sip that opens with a punch of melon and lingers with a hint of caramel and spice. Use a soft hand when pouring in the splash of bubbles; the wine opens up the flavors, but be careful not to drown out the drink's softer notes with too much liquid.

In a mixing tin filled with ice, combine the tequila, pineapple juice, Midori, lime juice, and simple syrup. Shake well until very cold, then strain in a wine glass filled with ice. Add a splash of sparkling wine and garnish with the orange wheel.

STARLIT

MAKES 1 DRINK

1½ ounces Ilegal Mezcal Joven

½ ounce The Bitter Truth
Golden Falernum liqueur

1 ounce fresh carrot juice

½ ounce fresh pineapple juice

½ ounce fresh lime juice

½ ounce honey syrup
(see page 165)

Chilled sparkling wine, to top

Sometimes, after taking a first sip of a cocktail, I can only say, "Okay, *wow*." Make Trevor Easton Langer's Starlit and see if you don't have the same reaction. Its bright orange hue all but invites you to drink it in. The aptly named Starlit captures mezcal's smoky mystique. The other flavors (carrot and pineapple's sweetness, lime's tang, falernum's spice) sit in jaunty contrast to the whiff of campfire embers. Falernum is a spiced liqueur originally from Barbados; made with ginger, clove, lime, and almonds, it is an essential component to tiki cocktails. This is a drink that sparks conversations.

In a cocktail shaker filled with ice, combine the mezcal, falernum, carrot juice, pineapple juice, lime juice, and honey syrup. Shake well until very cold. Strain into a coupe and top with sparkling wine.

MIMOSA 2.0

MAKES 1 DRINK

1½ ounces yogurt soju, preferably Jinro soju

1 ounce Orange Oleo Saccharum (recipe follows)

1 ounce Calpico

3 ounces well-chilled dry Prosecco

Dehydrated orange wheel, for garnish

The mimosa (as well as its sister, the Bellini) is among the most famous Champagne cocktails and is synonymous with daytime celebrations and leisurely weekend brunches. In this very elegant update, Momofuku's acclaimed beverage director Haera Shin teases out the drink's vibrant aromatics, burnishing orange's sharp edges with a silky soju and the complementary zing of Calpico.

Calpico is a popular milk-based Japanese beverage and can be found in most Asian grocery stores. Be sure to use the original flavor, which is not carbonated. Yogurt soju is found at specialty liquor stores as well as online; if you can't locate it, a "fresh" or "chamisul" soju such as Jinro Chamisul is a viable stand-in.

In a mixing tin filled with ice, combine the soju, oleo saccharum, and Calpico. Shake well to combine, then strain into a wine glass filled with ice. Top with the Prosecco and garnish with the dehydrated orange wheel.

ORANGE OLEO SACCHARUM

MAKES ABOUT 1 CUP

1 cup sugar

⅓ cup orange peels (from about 1 orange; bitter pith cut away)

7 ounces orange juice (from 3 to 4 oranges, depending on size)

In a high-speed blender or food processor, combine the sugar, orange peels, and orange juice and blend for 1 minute. Strain through a conical strainer or chef's linen and discard the solids. Store in an airtight container in the refrigerator for 2 to 3 days.

HEARTBREAKER ROYALE

MAKES 1 DRINK

1 ounce vodka

½ ounce Giffard Crème de Pamplemousse Rose liqueur

½ ounce fresh lime juice

½ ounce fresh grapefruit juice

Chilled Champagne, to top

1 dash Bittercube Jamaican No. 1 bitters

Long strip of grapefruit peel, for garnish

You'll always remember the first time you laid eyes on the Heartbreaker Royale. Bar star turned ready-to-drink entrepreneur Aaron Polsky whips up this spiced grapefruit concoction that is light and playful yet envelops you in a seductive aroma of cloves and allspice. Think of Bittercube's Jamaican No. 1 bitters as tying the drink together with an elegant bow. Crafted by a small-batch bartender-beloved brand, the bitters are made with ginger, allspice, and lavender for a peppery, lush experience. This recipe makes one drink, but if you'd like to prepare it for a group, see the note below.

In a cocktail shaker filled with ice, combine the vodka, crème de pamplemousse, lime juice, and grapefruit juice and shake until frothy and cold. Strain into a collins glass filled with ice. Top with the Champagne and the bitters, and garnish with the grapefruit peel.

NOTE

To batch-prepare this cocktail for a group, multiply all the ingredients except for the bitters and Champagne, and combine in a pitcher a few hours before you want to serve. When ready to serve, simply pour the mixture into collins glasses over ice, then top each with Champagne and a dash of bitters and garnish as you would for an individual serving.

MIDNIGHT STARS

MAKES 1 DRINK

2 ounces chilled Fever-Tree Sparkling Sicilian Lemonade

2 ounces chilled Black Metallic Sweet Tea (recipe follows)

2 ounces chilled Veuve Clicquot Rich Champagne

Lemon slice, for garnish

I discovered August Uncommon, a small-batch California-based artisanal tea maker, while sourcing recipes for my first book on alcohol-free drinks, and I've been a loyal customer since. Every tea features culinary-inspired combinations, intense flavors, and romantic, evocative product descriptions ("feels like stargazing on an empty beach," "feels like a brisk walk under a harvest moon"). August Uncommon teas are my go-tos for developing original drinks, because they deliver a wallop of nuanced flavor without added sugars or alcohol. This drink showcases their Black Metallic, an expressive, floral black tea with notes of candied violet, elderberry, blackberry, and incense.

An Arnold Palmer–inspired drink, the Midnight Stars pairs a strongly brewed black tea with Fever-Tree's fantastic lemonade mixer and Veuve Clicquot Rich, a Champagne designed for use in cocktails.

In a highball glass filled with ice, combine the lemonade, sweet tea, and Champagne. Stir once to combine. Garnish with the lemon slice.

BLACK METALLIC SWEET TEA
MAKES 16 OUNCES

2 cups boiling water

2 tablespoons loose August Uncommon Black Metallic violet-elderberry tea

1 tablespoon simple syrup (see page 168)

In a 1-quart container, combine the boiling water, tea, and simple syrup. Let steep for at least 10 minutes for a strong brew. Strain the tea through a fine-mesh strainer and discard the solids. Store in an airtight container in the refrigerator for 3 to 5 days.

THE BALLERINO

MAKES 1 DRINK

1 ounce Angel's Envy
bourbon

1 ounce St-Germain
elderflower liqueur

1 ounce ginger-lemon
kombucha, such as
Health-Ade

2 drops Bittercube Jamaican
No. 1 Bitters

2 ounces chilled
sparkling wine

Micro blossom confetti,
for garnish

American Ballet Theatre principal dancer James
Whiteside is the inspiration behind Earlecia Gibb's
The Ballerino, a cocktail that gambols gracefully
across various flavor profiles. A high-quality Kentucky
bourbon, specifically Angel's Envy, which is finished
in port wine barrels, introduces vanilla and caramel
tones that unfurl in the bouquet and linger through the
finish. The St-Germain and kombucha add a harmony
of sweetness and citrus, while the Bittercube Jamaican
No. 1 bitters are essential for an extra note of melodious
warmth. The splash of sparkling wine bubbles, which
opens up the whiskey's flavors, adds a satisfying coda.
Micro blossoms are edible flowers; they can be purchased
at specialty food stores.

In a wine glass filled with ice, combine the bourbon,
St-Germain, kombucha, and bitters. Top with sparkling
wine. Garnish with a sprinkling of micro blossom confetti.

AN ITALIAN AFTERNOON
IN THE GROVE

MAKES 1 DRINK

1 ounce Cocchi Americano Bianco (see page 9)

½ ounce Italicus Rosolio di Bergamotto liqueur

¼ ounce Aperol

Chilled Prosecco, to top

1 drop orange blossom water (optional)

There are few drinks more aptly named than Brooks Moyer's An Italian Afternoon in the Grove. The all-Italian ingredients are redolent of lush florals and juicy citrus. This is an Italian summer day, captured in a glass.

Orange blossom water, like absinthe, delivers a lot of fragrance and flavor even in tiny amounts and can be divisive. That said, orange blossom water ties this cocktail experience together, acting as a distinctively shimmery aromatic that unites the other flavors.

In a wine glass filled with ice, combine the Cocchi Americano, Italicus, and Aperol. Stir to combine, then top with Prosecco. Finish with the orange blossom water, if desired.

NOTE

Even a few drops of orange blossom water can seem overwhelmingly perfume-y; to ensure that you add just a small drop to your cocktail, use an eyedropper, or pour a dash into a ⅛-teaspoon measuring spoon first, then add it to the glass.

SPREZZATURA

MAKES 1 DRINK

1 ounce Garden Basilcello
(recipe follows)

½ ounce fresh lemon juice

½ ounce simple syrup
(see page 168)

2 ounces chilled Fever-Tree
Sparkling Lime & Yuzu soda

Chilled Prosecco, to top

Sprig of basil, for garnish

Sprezzatura is an Italian term that means "artful nonchalance." It's casually throwing things together, seemingly without effort, but the result is always graceful. In other words, it's the art of not trying too hard. Basilcello (and its cousin, limoncello) is a perfect example of this: transforming an infusion of garden-fresh herbs into a charmingly citrusy, herbaceous drink with a gentle, savory finish.

Even though the basilcello is made with vodka, this aromatic drink will appeal to both the vodka-soda crowd and fussy gin-and-tonic aficionados due to its earthy garden flavors.

In a mixing tin filled with ice, combine the basilcello, lemon juice, and simple syrup. Shake briskly until very cold. Strain into a highball glass filled with ice. Add the lime-yuzu soda, then top with Prosecco. Garnish with the basil.

GARDEN BASILCELLO

MAKES ABOUT 18 OUNCES

16 ounces vodka

4 cups loosely packed fresh basil (including stems)

½ cup boiling water

½ cup sugar

½ teaspoon citric acid

Letting this mixture infuse for a full day results in a fragrant, gorgeous chartreuse liquid. Don't be intimidated by the strong herbal flavor; when diluted in a drink, it truly shines. In Italy, basilcello (like limoncello) is served alone as a palate-cleansing shot during or after dinner courses, but can also be mixed with sparkling lemonade or tonic.

In a 1-quart container, combine the vodka and basil. Cover and set aside at room temperature to infuse for 24 hours (or up to a week for a stronger flavor).

Strain into a glass or plastic container with a lid and discard the solids.

In a small container, combine the boiling water, sugar, and citric acid and stir until the sugar has dissolved. Add the mixture to the strained vodka and stir to combine. Cover and store in the refrigerator or freezer for up to 2 months; the natural color will begin to fade after 1 to 2 weeks.

BEAUTIFUL STRANGER

MAKES 1 DRINK

1½ ounces tequila blanco

¾ ounce fresh lemon juice

¾ ounce grenadine

Chilled Champagne or
sparkling wine, to top

Lemon twist, for garnish

If we drink with our eyes, then this smashing pink cocktail is love at first sight. Acclaimed San Diego bartender Erick Castro is a master of coaxing vibrant flavors out of a minimalist set of ingredients. In the Beautiful Stranger, grenadine and lemon juice provide a memorable pop of color and sweetness, while tequila gives the drink a lingering soft finish that will have guests clamoring for another round.

In a cocktail shaker filled with ice, combine the tequila, lemon juice, and grenadine. Shake briskly until well chilled, then strain into a flute. Top with Champagne and garnish with the lemon twist.

CHAMPAGNE RAMOS

MAKES 1 DRINK

1½ ounces Beefeater gin

1 ounce orgeat

¼ ounce fresh lemon juice

1 ounce burrata water
(see headnote)

Chilled Champagne, to top

Toasted almonds, for
garnish

Edible glitter, for garnish

A Ramos gin fizz is one of the most famous "eye-openers," a category of classic drinks designed to ease you into the day after a night of carousing. The traditional Ramos is made with egg white, orange blossom water, and seltzer. Its instructions, made famous in New Orleans, require up to 12 minutes of straight shaking. A hated-but-beloved bar staple, the Ramos gin fizz continues to inspire bartenders who crave the ethereal lightness of the drink but want to skip the exhausting prep.

At New York's Dante, a frequent World's 50 Best Bars winner, the Ramos gets a fresh update: Burrata water (the milky water in which fresh burrata cheese is packaged) is swapped in for egg whites, while orgeat plays a lovely harmony against a fragrant London dry-style gin. The burrata gives the drink a creamy frothiness and body; chilling the drink in the freezer builds a meringue-like fizz that rises to the top when the last splash of Champagne is poured in.

Use a short highball
when making this drink
to avoid overdiluting
the cocktail's soft notes
with too much wine.

In a cocktail shaker filled with ice, combine the gin, orgeat, lemon juice, and burrata water. Shake until the mixture is well chilled and the ice is broken up. You should end up with a nice froth.

Strain into a short highball glass. Add a little bit of Champagne, then place in the freezer for a full minute. Remove the glass from the freezer, then slowly pour additional Champagne to the top of the glass. Garnish with toasted almonds and edible glitter.

COSMO SPRITZ

MAKES 1 DRINK

¾ ounce Absolut Citron vodka

¾ ounce Lillet Rosé (see page 9)

¾ ounce cranberry juice

½ ounce Cointreau

½ ounce fresh lime juice

2 ounces chilled Perrier-Jouët Grand Brut Champagne

3 green grapes skewered with a cocktail pick, for garnish

Come through, Cosmopolitan. The drink that launched a thousand girls' nights gets the royale treatment. In Jane Danger's riff, the classic recipe is lifted with a kiss of Lillet Rosé, the iconic French aperitif, and finished with a smattering of twinkling bubbles. Spirited and insouciant, this is a drink that easily floats from day into night.

In a footed wine glass filled with ice, combine the vodka, Lillet, cranberry juice, Cointreau, and lime juice. Stir well to combine. Top with the Champagne and garnish with the grapes.

FRENCH KISS

MAKES 1 DRINK

1 ounce Citadelle gin

½ ounce fresh lemon juice

¼ ounce simple syrup
(see page 168)

¼ ounce Giffard Rhubarbe
liqueur

1 dash absinthe

Chilled sparkling wine,
to top

Lemon twist, for garnish

Natasha David is one of the bartending world's most celebrated stars, and for good reason. A typical Natasha David cocktail alchemizes recognizable flavors into a wholly new experience that almost defies categorization. In her French Kiss, the gin, lemon, rhubarb liqueur, and absinthe—each identifiable flavors on their own—meld into something greater than the sum of the drink's parts. A lilting citrus bouquet cedes to an elegant sip that sits dry on the palate, with a finish that glides just above savory. Absinthe imbues the drink with an alluring pearlescent appearance and a savory hint.

In a cocktail shaker filled with ice, combine the gin, lemon juice, simple syrup, rhubarb liqueur, and absinthe. Shake briskly until well chilled. Double strain into a coupe, then slowly top with sparkling wine. Garnish with the lemon twist.

NOTE

In order to prevent the absinthe from overwhelming the drink, attach a pour spout to your absinthe bottle (which helps control how much liquid comes out) or, preferably, use an eyedropper to add just a dash to your drink. In other words, in this recipe, treat absinthe like you would bitters, where a little goes a long way.

INSTANT CRUSH

MAKES 1 DRINK

1½ ounces blanco tequila, such as Espolon

½ ounce Yuzuri yuzu liqueur

½ ounce simple syrup (see page 168)

2 ounces chilled sparkling wine

2 ounces chilled Fever-Tree Sparkling Lime & Yuzu soda

Lime wheel, for garnish

Ranch water is a drink that's exploded in popularity in recent years. A simple three-ingredient mix of blanco tequila, lime juice, and sparkling mineral water, ranch water is imminently suited to benefit from a sprinkling of sparkling bubbles. A typical ranch water cocktail, however, does not have sugar, which proves too acidic when combined with sparkling wine.

Zigging away from the original recipe, I upped the citrus notes by introducing yuzu, while also softening those zingy edges with a hint of sweetness. A bracingly cold Fever-Tree Sparkling Lime & Yuzu soda brings in a touch of lime (a nod to the original recipe) while also maintaining the drink's fizzy appeal. Serve with the Fever-Tree bottle on the side so guests can extend their drink as they like. (The name, Instant Crush, is a nod to both the Daft Punk–Julian Casablancas song and the drink's sessionable qualities.)

In a highball glass filled with ice, combine the tequila, Yuzuri, and simple syrup. Stir briskly to combine; add more ice, if needed. Slowly add the sparkling wine, then add the lime-yuzu soda. Garnish with the lime wheel. Serve with the bottle of Fever-Tree on the side so your guest can top off their drink.

ISLA BONITA

MAKES 1 DRINK

1½ ounces white rum

¾ ounce fresh lemon juice

¾ ounce raspberry syrup, homemade (see page 166) or store-bought

2 dashes Peychaud's bitters

Chilled sparkling rosé wine, to top

Grapefruit twist, for garnish

This lithesome rum drink is buoyed by the sweetness of raspberries on one side and the acidity of sparkling wine on the other. Neither cloyingly sweet nor dryly acidic, Erick Castro's Isla Bonita has the mass appeal of a limpid sunny day and will transport you to the island bar of your dreams.

While you can easily purchase raspberry syrup at a specialty store, consider putting in about an hour's work to make the syrup fresh.

In a cocktail shaker filled with ice, combine the rum, lemon juice, raspberry syrup, and bitters. Shake briskly until well chilled, then strain into a coupe. Top with sparkling wine and garnish with the grapefruit twist.

LA FAVORITE

MAKES 1 DRINK

½ ounce Bénédictine

½ ounce fresh lemon juice

½ ounce honey syrup
(see page 165)

2½ ounces well-chilled
Moët & Chandon Rosé
Impérial Champagne

A heady, aromatic liqueur made from a secret recipe of citrus, honey, and spices, Bénédictine reportedly dates back to 1510. In La Favorite, a whisper of honey brings the complexity of Bénédictine to the fore. Lush and sophisticated, one sip will call forth visions of silk georgette ball gowns sweeping across marble floors or post-midnight encounters in candlelit bars.

In a cocktail shaker filled with ice, combine the Bénédictine, lemon juice, and honey syrup. Shake vigorously. Strain into a flute and top with the Champagne.

SBAGLIATO SICILIA

MAKES 1 DRINK

¾ ounce Luxardo Bitter Bianco liqueur

¾ ounce Dolin Blanc vermouth

½ ounce limoncello, homemade (see page 163) or store-bought

2 dashes lemon bitters

2½ ounces well-chilled Prosecco

½ ounce well-chilled S.Pellegrino mineral water

Edible borage flowers, for garnish

The Negroni has spawned endless variations, including the popular "White Negroni." (In a White Negroni, the ingredients are primarily clear or golden-hued, such as Suze and Lillet Blanc, as opposed to the traditional recipe, which features Campari's signature red liquid.) It follows that Negroni's sparkling little sister, the Sbagliato, will also thrive from endless makeovers, each more sprightly than the last.

A bestseller at Manhattan's Dante, the Sbagliato Sicilia is a riff on the White Negroni. Linden Pride's team engineered a drink where the strident zing of limoncello tempers the herbaceous Luxardo and savory Dolin Blanc, resulting in a brisk and refreshingly grown-up drink that lingers with a distractingly delectable finish.

In a highball glass filled with ice, combine the Luxardo, Dolin Blanc, limoncello, lemon bitters, Prosecco, and mineral water and stir gently to combine. Garnish with edible flowers.

FLOREALE SPRITZ

MAKES 1 DRINK

3 ounces Martini & Rossi
Floreale nonalcoholic
vermouth

2 ounces chilled Prosecco,
preferably Martini & Rossi

1 ounce chilled soda water

Lemon wheel, for garnish

Even though the Floreale
is nonalcoholic, think
of it like a wine aperitif
or a vermouth. As such,
once opened, it must be
refrigerated.

The rise of the sober-curious movement has resulted in a broad new category of sophisticated nonalcoholic mixers. A non-alc mixer, especially one that's packed with layered, nuanced flavors, is a great way to introduce complexity to drinks while also keeping alcoholic content low overall. It's a hostess's secret weapon: a way to keep the party going without the worry of overserving your guests.

Martini & Rossi's nonalcoholic white vermouth, Floreale, features chamomile and a hint of bitterness that plays well against the sparkling wine. Martini & Rossi also make a nonalcoholic mixer with bergamot and citrus notes called Vibrante, which can be substituted for the Floreale in this recipe in the same proportion.

Fill a balloon glass with ice. Pour the Floreale and Prosecco directly into the glass. Top with the soda water. Stir gently for a few moments, then garnish with the lemon wheel.

IN BLOOM

MAKES 1 DRINK

2 ounces chilled rosé hard apple cider, preferably Right Bee Cider

2 ounces chilled sparkling rosé wine, preferably Veuve Clicquot Rosé Champagne

1 ounce Aperol

Hard fruit ciders are a great addition to cocktails because they provide a pop of flavor and effervescence without weighing down wine's profile. Rosé hard apple cider variations, produced by craft brewers as well as local wineries, are pretty easy to find, especially during the warm months. In this drink, rosé apple cider from a craft Chicago brewery and Aperol combine to make a fizzy blush-orange cocktail that's ready for its social media moment.

In a balloon glass filled with ice, combine the cider, sparkling wine, and Aperol. Stir once to combine.

MAROON FIVE

MAKES 1 DRINK

2 ounces Hibiscus Water
(recipe follows)

1 ounce Lo-Fi Aperitifs
gentian amaro

½ ounce Cerasum Aperitivo

½ ounce Fords sloe gin

½ ounce fresh lemon juice

Chilled Lambrusco, to top

When all but one ingredient is a deep scarlet, the resulting cocktail is sure to be as eye-catching as a perfectly applied crimson lip. The tart zing of hibiscus and lemon underlines the savory bitterness of gentian amaro and the sweetness of cherry and sloeberry. Cerasum Aperitivo's recipe is over one hundred years old (dating to 1906) and features a blend of three different berries, sakura (cherry blossoms), and herbs. Lambrusco, a darkly luscious sparkling Italian red wine, adds the perfect finish and keeps the drink from dipping into cloying sweetness. Sloe gin, popular in the UK, is characterized by a balance of sweet, tart, and spicy.

In a cocktail shaker filled with ice, combine the hibiscus water, amaro, Cerasum, sloe gin, and lemon juice. Shake until well chilled and frothy. Strain into a highball glass filled with ice. Top with Lambrusco and serve.

HIBISCUS WATER

MAKES 28 TO 30 OUNCES

1 cup dried hibiscus flowers

32 ounces boiling water

In a 1-quart container, combine the hibiscus flowers and water. Set aside to steep at room temperature for at least 3 hours or up to overnight (for a stronger flavor).

Strain the hibiscus water into a clean container and discard the solids. Store in the refrigerator for up to 1 week.

LADY STONEHEART

MAKES 1 DRINK

½ ounce sweet vermouth, preferably Carpano Punt e Mes

1 teaspoon simple syrup (see page 168)

4 dashes Angostura bitters

Chilled Champagne, to top

Orange twist, for garnish

Easy to make and even easier to sip, Erick Castro's sweet-vermouth-and-bubbles sipper sits dry on the palate, with a soft botanical finish. Carpano Punt e Mes is a well-known Italian vermouth that you'll find in top bars everywhere; the name, according to its producer, refers to the liquid's "one point of sweetness and half a point of bitterness." With its soft hints of orange and intriguing herbal flourish, Lady Stoneheart's layered flavors come to life with a kiss of sparkling effervescence.

In a flute or wine glass filled with ice, combine the vermouth, simple syrup, and bitters. Stir to combine. Top with the Champagne and garnish with the orange twist.

MAS MOJITO

MAKES 1 DRINK

1½ ounces
Zacapa No. 23 rum

½ ounce fresh lime juice

1 teaspoon brown sugar

Handful of fresh mint

¾ ounce chilled Champagne
or sparkling wine, to top

Mint sprig, for garnish
(optional)

The mojito, a warm-weather classic, gets a well-deserved royale treatment in this recipe: Jaunty bubbles play well against the fresh mint's herbaceousness and the dark rum's velvety sweetness, delivering a drink that evokes cerulean skies and neon nights.

In a cocktail shaker filled with ice, combine the rum, lime juice, brown sugar, and mint. Shake well until very cold and well combined. Strain into a highball glass filled with ice and top with the Champagne. Garnish with the mint sprig, if desired.

SGROPPINO SBAGLIATO

MAKES 1 DRINK

2 ounces French sweet
vermouth, preferably Lillet
Rouge

¾ ounce Campari

1 scoop high-quality citrus
sorbet, preferably Sharon's
Sorbet lemon sorbet

2 ounces brut Champagne,
preferably G.H. Mumm
Grand Cordon

Edible glitter, for garnish
(optional)

Much like when two mega pop stars join forces to create the collab of their fans' dreams, Jane Danger has created a cocktail mash-up of two iconic Italian drinks: the Negroni Sbagliato and the Sgroppino, a famed Venetian dessert cocktail made by combining vodka, lemon sorbet, and Prosecco. Whimsical and delicious, look for Campari's signature bitterness balanced by a piquant-yet-sweet lemon bite and a subtle fizz in every sip.

In a mixing glass filled with ice, combine the vermouth and Campari. Stir briskly for at least 30 seconds, until well chilled. Strain into a coupe. Add a scoop of sorbet, then slowly pour the Champagne into the glass around the sorbet. Garnish with edible glitter, if desired.

SPRING BREAKERS

MAKES 1 DRINK

Flaky sea salt, chile salt, smoked black salt, or Himalayan pink salt, for rimming the glass (optional; see Note)

Lime wedge, for rimming the glass, plus 1 lime wheel for garnish (optional)

1 ounce tequila, preferably Volcan de Mi Tierra blanco or reposado

1½ ounces fresh watermelon juice

½ ounce fresh lime juice

½ ounce simple syrup (see page 168)

Chilled brut sparkling wine, preferably rosé, to top

Watermelon wedge, for garnish (optional)

A watermelon margarita, but make it bubbly. This is a straightforward adaptation of the world's most beloved cocktail: Take a margarita, then add fresh watermelon and a flourish of crisp, dry bubbles. I personally love the depth that reposado tequilas bring to margaritas, but a blanco tequila will do just fine in this drink with built-in mass appeal.

Spread salt over a small plate. Run a lime wedge around the rim of a coupe to wet it, then dip it in the salt to coat.

In a mixing tin, combine the tequila, watermelon juice, lime juice, and simple syrup. Add ice and shake vigorously until very cold. Fill the salt-rimmed coupe with ice and strain the drink into the glass. Top with sparkling wine. Garnish with the watermelon or lime wheel, if desired.

 NOTE

Instead of rimming the glass with salt, you can also coat half a lime wheel with salt and use that as a garnish instead.

For a slightly drier take, reduce the simple syrup to ¼ ounce.

VICE VERSA

MAKES 1 DRINK

1 ounce gin, preferably New York Distilling Company Dorothy Parker gin

¾ ounce fresh grapefruit juice

½ ounce Giffard Crème de Pamplemousse Rose liqueur

½ ounce Luxardo Bitter Rosso liqueur

2 ounces chilled dry rosé Cava, such as Raventós i Blanc

No exaggeration: Meaghan Dorman's Vice Versa is at the top of my list of favorite cocktails ever. The drink showcases the best qualities of its components: the floral notes of a contemporary-style craft gin, the lively zing of grapefruit, the insouciance of rosé bubbles. Appropriate for that post-work golden hour as well as a cheeky midnight nightcap, this is a drink that shimmers with sophistication.

In a cocktail shaker, combine the gin, grapefruit juice, crème de pamplemousse, and Luxardo. Add ice and shake well. Strain into a flute or coupe. Top with the rosé Cava.

CHELSEA MORNING

MAKES 1 DRINK

¾ ounce chilled white peach puree, preferably The Perfect Purée

½ ounce chilled lychee puree, preferably The Perfect Purée

½ ounce chilled Jasmine Tea Syrup (recipe follows)

¼ ounce chilled Hojun yuzu sake

1 teaspoon chilled Giffard Lichi-Li lychee liqueur

4 ounces chilled Grandial blanc de blancs or other Champagne

Apple blossom, for garnish

The Bellini, a glamorous mix of white peach and Prosecco, was invented in 1948 by Giuseppe Cipriani at Harry's Bar in Venice, Italy, and quickly became an enduring classic. Hotel Chelsea's Brian Evans, who has a reputation for bringing a discerning touch to modern classics, updates the Bellini with an infusion of Asian flavors, including lychee and jasmine.

Fruity but not cloying, fragrant yet still light on its feet, the Chelsea Morning infuses any occasion with Old World élan. Note that like the traditional Bellini, this cocktail is built in a glass without ice, so everything needs to be chilled before serving.

In a mixing glass or container, combine the peach puree, lychee puree, tea syrup, sake, and lychee liqueur. Stir to combine, then refrigerate until thoroughly chilled. Pour the chilled mixture directly into a wine glass. Top with the Champagne and garnish with the apple blossom.

JASMINE TEA SYRUP

MAKES 24 OUNCES

¼ cup Jasmine Dragon
Pearls green tea

23 ounces hot water

1 cup sugar

In a 1-quart container, combine the tea and hot water. Set aside to steep for 5 to 10 minutes. Meanwhile, place the sugar in a medium bowl. While the tea is still warm, strain it into the bowl over the sugar and stir until well combined (the heat of the tea will help dissolve the sugar). Transfer to an airtight container and store in the refrigerator for up to 1 week.

NOTE

To extend the life of the syrup, break it up into smaller containers and freeze it for up to 2 months. (This syrup is enchanting as a sweetener for teas as well as fruit smoothies. A little goes a long way.)

YOU ALWAYS REMEMBER
YOUR FIRST

MAKES 1 DRINK

1 ounce well-chilled
Lambrusco

1 ounce well-chilled Prosecco

½ ounce limoncello,
homemade (see page 163)
or store-bought

¼ ounce simple syrup
(see page 168)

2 dashes Hella Cocktail
Co. citrus bitters

Pebble ice, for serving

Handful of mint sprigs,
for garnish

In this delightful and easy-to-make recipe, longtime NYC bar owner Alyssa Sartor artfully combines two sparklers (Prosecco and Lambrusco), then ties them up with a pretty limoncello ribbon. Citrus-forward yet not too sweet, this cocktail hits the Venn diagram of desirable party drinks: flavorful and charming but also low ABV.

The drink is inspired by Alyssa's childhood memory of her Italian grandparents insisting that she try red wine when she was six years old. Her mother, reluctant to hand over a full glass of wine, diluted it with Sprite. Hence, the name: You Always Remember Your First.

In a rocks glass, combine the Lambrusco, Prosecco, limoncello, simple syrup, and bitters. Dry stir to combine. Top with pebble ice. Garnish with the mint.

UNDER THE CHERRY MOON

MAKES 1 DRINK

6 or more fresh Thai basil leaves or regular basil leaves

½ ounce tart cherry juice

½ ounce fresh lemon juice

½ ounce Licor 43 liqueur

Chilled Cava, to top

Tart and savory, Brooks Moyer's Under the Cherry Moon will turn heads with its deep ruby hue. Fresh basil leaves add an unexpected herbaceousness that tempers the zing of the cherry juice and also imbues the drink with an earthy finish. Licor 43, a Spanish liqueur made with vanilla, spices, and citrus fruits, is an inspired choice of sweetener, providing both candied notes and subtle acidity.

Tear up the basil leaves and place them in a cocktail shaker. Add the cherry juice, lemon juice, Licor 43, and ice. Hard shake to really bring out the basil flavor. Strain into a wine glass filled with ice, then top with chilled Cava.

EL REY

MAKES 1 DRINK

1 ounce mezcal

1 ounce Nixta Licor de Elote corn liqueur

¾ ounce fresh lemon juice

¼ ounce cinnamon syrup (see page 164)

2 ounces chilled dry sparkling wine, such as Conquilla Cava Brut

Rose water, in an atomizer

Dried rosebud, for garnish

The El Rey, created by the team at the Raines Law Room in New York City's Chelsea neighborhood, is a love letter to Mexican flavors, beginning with mezcal, which provides the base spirit for the drink. Nixta is a liqueur made from raw and roasted heirloom corn sweetened with piloncillo, an unrefined cane sugar, and whiskey. Cinnamon syrup and a kiss of rose water round out a flavor experience reminiscent of traditional Mexican pastries.

In a mixing tin filled with ice, combine the mezcal, Nixta Licor de Elote, lemon juice, and cinnamon syrup. Shake well to combine, then strain into a flute. Top with sparkling wine. Spritz the glass lightly with rose water and garnish with the dried rosebud.

CRAZY DIAMOND

MAKES 1 DRINK

1 ounce Paul Beau VS Cognac

½ ounce Hans Reisetbauer hazelnut eau-de-vie

¾ ounce strawberry syrup (see page 169)

½ ounce fresh lemon juice

1 teaspoon Luxardo Maraschino Originale liqueur

Chilled Champagne, to top

Strawberry, for garnish

Cognac is the perfect canvas to show off strawberry and hazelnut's innate compatibility. On its own, hazelnut is a favored pairing for Champagne because it highlights some of the wine's more subtle accents. When combined with strawberry, as it is in Tyson Buhler's concoction, it unfurls a heady aroma of nuttiness that's trailed by a lingering echo of summer-ripened fruits.

In a mixing tin filled with ice, combine the cognac, eau-de-vie, strawberry syrup, lemon juice, and maraschino liqueur. Shake well to combine. Double strain into a flute, then top slowly with chilled Champagne. Garnish with the strawberry.

EL ERROR

MAKES 1 DRINK

1½ ounces Granada-Vallet pomegranate amaro

1½ ounces Cocchi Americano Bianco

2½ ounces chilled tepache

3 ounces Mexican sparkling wine, preferably Terra Mädi Blanc de Noirs

Orange slice dipped in chamoy, for garnish

Even in a city that's in touch with its Mexican heritage, Los Angeles's Maxwell Reis is unparalleled in his expertise on Mexico's distilling heritage, gained through years of frequent visits with small distillers and producers. The El Error, an homage to the Negroni Sbagliato, features almost exclusively Mexican ingredients. Of particular note: Granada-Vallet, a Mexican bitter pomegranate liqueur, alludes to Italy's Campari yet delivers a complexity and luscious color of its own merit. Tepache, a fermented pineapple drink, and chamoy, a savory Mexican condiment made from pickled fruits, are found in most grocery stores. According to Max, "Granada-Vallet's bitter pomegranate flavor is brightened by the acidity and funk of the tepache, and candied by the blanc vermouth. The addition of the Mexican sparkling wine completes the tip of the 'sombrero' to the classic Sbagliato, and makes it a refreshing cocktail for any time of day."

In a wine glass filled with ice, combine the amaro, Cocchi, tepache, and sparkling wine. Stir quickly to combine. Garnish with the chamoy-dipped orange slice.

FLEUR SAUVAGE

MAKES 1 DRINK

1 ounce Bombay Bramble gin

¾ ounce St-Germain elderflower liqueur

1 ounce lychee juice (see Note)

¼ ounce fresh lime juice

Chilled sparkling rosé wine, to top

A sun-drenched garden party comes to life in the Fleur Sauvage. Designed by St-Germain ambassador Earlecia Gibb, the drink is a bouquet of floral and fruit notes, including lychee, blackberry, and elderflower, arranged into a blush-tinted sip that's sure to be the talk of any gathering. Make an effort to use Bombay's ruby-toned Bramble expression, which infuses the drink with color as well as vibrant fruit and botanical accents.

In a cocktail shaker filled with ice, combine the gin, elderflower liqueur, lychee juice, and lime juice. Shake until well combined. Strain into a flute and top with sparkling rosé.

NOTE

To make lychee juice, blend one 20-ounce can seedless lychees in syrup until smooth. Strain through a fine-mesh strainer into an airtight container. Store in the refrigerator for up to 2 weeks.

FLUFFY MARGARITA ROYALE

MAKES 1 DRINK

Hawaiian lava salt, for rimming and garnish (optional)

1 lime wedge, for rimming the glass (optional)

1½ ounces Olmeca Altos blanco tequila

½ ounce Pierre Ferrand dry curaçao

¾ ounce Saffron and Clementine Syrup (recipe follows)

¾ ounce fresh lime juice

1½ ounces chilled Prosecco

2 ounces fluffy clementine juice (see Note)

Clementine wedge, for garnish

Is there anything more enticing than a margarita with fresh juice *and* sparkling wine? The world-famous bar team at Dante created this gorgeously layered margarita, which features fresh clementine juice and sparkling wine as a callback to the mimosa. Saffron adds a savory undertone that lingers with tequila's agave finish. Finished with fresh clementine juice, this is two of the world's most popular drinks combined in one irresistible sip.

Spread salt over a small plate. Run the lime wedge halfway around the rim of a spritz tumbler or a double rocks glass to wet it and dip it in the salt to coat. Add ice to the glass, then add the tequila, curaçao, syrup, lime juice, and Prosecco. Stir to combine. Top with the clementine juice and garnish with the clementine wedge, dipped in lava salt, if desired.

NOTE

The juice drinks at Dante are famous for their "fluffiness," which occurs when fruits are processed on-demand through a Breville juicer. To achieve max fluffiness at home, juice the fruits just before using and do not strain away any of the resulting "fluff," or frothy head, that naturally occurs.

SAFFRON AND CLEMENTINE SYRUP

MAKES ABOUT 17 OUNCES

2½ cups sugar

14 ounces Acqua Panna mineral water

Large pinch of saffron threads

Peel of 2 clementines

In a small saucepan, combine the sugar and mineral water and warm over low heat until the sugar has dissolved, about 5 minutes. Pour the syrup into a clean container and add the saffron and clementine peels. Refrigerate overnight to infuse.

Strain the syrup into a fresh bottle and seal; discard the solids. Store in the refrigerator for up to 1 week.

GINGER SPRITZ

MAKES 1 DRINK

1½ ounces chilled Lillet Blanc (see page 9)

½ ounce ginger liqueur, preferably Domaine de Canton

1 ounce chilled Campo Viejo Cava Brut Reserva

1 ounce chilled club soda, preferably Fever-Tree

2 dashes lime bitters

Orange half-wheel, for garnish

An effortless drink with a lively presence, Jane Danger's Ginger Spritz is in the running to be your go-to sip when you want something that's a touch drier than an Aperol Spritz but still squarely in the Light & Refreshing category. For best results, chill as many of the ingredients (the Lillet, Cava, and club soda) as possible to bracingly cold temperatures before serving.

In a wine glass filled with ice, combine the Lillet, ginger liqueur, Cava, club soda, and bitters, then stir once to combine. Garnish with the orange half-wheel in the glass.

GLAMAZONIAN AIRWAYS

MAKES 1 DRINK

¾ ounce Plantation Stiggins' Fancy Pineapple rum

¼ ounce Jack From Brooklyn Sorel liqueur (see Note)

½ ounce fresh lime juice

½ ounce Black Cardamom Syrup (recipe follows)

1½ ounces brut sparkling wine, such as Poema Cava Brut

Edible glitter stars, for garnish

Joyface's Ben Hopkins brings a playful and inventive artistry to his drinks—his Glamazonian Airways is a perfect example. Named in reference to *RuPaul's Drag Race*, the cocktail is a transportive experience. One sip of its tropical headiness conjures up visions of sun-drenched beaches and the soothing murmur of waves crashing at midnight. Seek out Plantation Rum's pineapple expression, which contributes a caramelized base note that other rums don't match. Ben's Black Cardamom Syrup will surprise you with a dusky smokiness reminiscent of peaty Scotch; you'll find it is a smashing sweetener in coffee and black teas.

In a mixing tin filled with ice, combine the rum, sorel liqueur, lime juice, and cardamom syrup. Shake briskly to combine, then add the sparkling wine to the tin and double strain into a coupe. Garnish with a sprinkling of edible glitter stars.

NOTE

Jack From Brooklyn Sorel is a small-batch hibiscus liqueur and tends to sell out. If you can't find Sorel, you can substitute Pama pomegranate liqueur, which is also ruby-toned and has a similar flavor profile.

BLACK CARDAMOM SYRUP

MAKES ABOUT 10 OUNCES

1 tablespoon (10 g) black cardamom pods, lightly crushed

11½ ounces simple syrup (see page 168)

Place an immersion circulator in a water bath and heat the water to 145°F. In a 1-quart container, combine the crushed cardamom pods and simple syrup. Seal the container and place it in the water bath. Cook for 2 hours. (If you don't own an immersion circulator, line a medium pot with a dish towel and fill with water. Submerge the container with the cardamom and simple syrup in the water heated to 145°F and cook for 2 hours.) Let cool to room temperature, then strain the syrup and discard the solids. Store in an airtight container in the refrigerator; the syrup will keep for about 2 weeks.

LE MARAIS

MAKES 1 DRINK

¾ ounce Suze herbal liqueur

Chilled Veuve Clicquot Brut Yellow Label Champagne

Lemon twist

Taking inspiration from the minimalist perfection of the Kir Royale (see page 27), this royale puts Suze, one of my all-time-favorite liqueurs, on a pedestal. Suze is a storied liqueur dating to 1889, made with an infusion of gentian, floral, and citrus ingredients. Exquisitely French (as noted in this recipe's name, which is that of my favorite neighborhood in Paris), all this drink needs is a lemon twist expressed across the top like an aromatic citrus ribbon.

Pour the Suze into a flute. Top with the Champagne. Express the oils from the lemon twist over the top of the drink, then run the twist around the rim of the glass before discarding.

I FOLLOW RIVERS

MAKES 1 DRINK

1½ ounces aged rum

½ ounce fresh lemon juice

¼ ounce alpine amaro (preferably Brucato Chaparral amaro or Yellow Chartreuse; see headnote)

¼ ounce crème de pêche liqueur

¼ ounce simple syrup (see page 168)

2 dashes Hella Cocktail Co. eucalyptus bitters

1½ ounces chilled Cava

Eucalyptus sprig, for garnish

With the premiere of Netflix's *Drinks Masters*, reality cooking competition shows got the craft cocktail upgrade that bar fans have long asked for. Fan favorite Christian "Suzu" Suzuki-Orellana instantly stood out, not just for his warm, likable persona but for a masterful cocktail technique informed by his Asian American heritage. In I Follow Rivers, Suzu layers flavors in a distinctly culinary way: Herbal tones blend into the honeyed notes of peach and aged rum, while a whisper of eucalyptus morphs into a savory flourish that emerges after each sip. Alpine amari is a broad category of liqueurs produced from mountain-grown botanicals such as juniper, genepy, and pine; in this case, Suzu recommends a California amaro made with yerba santa and spearmint, or Yellow Chartreuse, the vegetal and herbaceous spirit distilled by monks.

In a mixing tin filled with ice, combine the rum, lemon juice, alpine liqueur, crème de pêche, simple syrup, and bitters. Shake briskly to combine. Double strain into a coupe, then top with the Cava. Garnish with the eucalyptus.

LUINI SPRITZ

MAKES 1 DRINK

¾ ounce Cynar

1¼ ounces amaretto liqueur

2 ounces chilled ginger beer

1½ ounces chilled Prosecco

With its caramelized-almond tones and lingering, savory finish, Daniel Sabo's Luini Spritz is instantly memorable. Evocative of an old-fashioned soda pop yet also sophisticated and breezy, this drink sings of languid summer afternoons and cozy winter hangouts. Nuanced yet also versatile, it's a spritz that can shine on multiple occasions and alongside a range of food pairings. Try it with Truffle Butter Popcorn (page 148) for an elevated take on a movie-night snack.

In a highball glass filled with ice, add all the ingredients, then stir gently to combine.

MÁ PÊCHE

. . . .

MAKES 1 DRINK

1 ounce Jasmine Tea Gin
(recipe follows)

1 ounce Jinro peach soju

½ ounce Choya Umeshu
liqueur

¼ ounce citric acid solution
(see page 171)

3 ounces crémant
sparkling wine

Edible flowers and FireStix,
for garnish

Mini clothespin, for garnish
(optional)

Lilting and fresh, Haera Shin's Asian-influenced
sparkling highball is a nuanced tapestry of citrus and
floral notes, opening with a bright acidity that cedes to
a subtle echo of jasmine and juniper.

It might seem decadent to infuse one full bottle
of gin with tea, as this recipe calls for, but it's a
common method craft bars use to introduce an added
dimension of complexity to spirits. Once infused, the
flavor will linger indefinitely. The jasmine-scented gin,
for example, will add bewitching notes to martinis,
highballs, and French 75s (see page 18), as well as to
this sparkling cocktail.

. . . .

In a mixing glass filled with ice, combine the gin, soju,
umeshu, and citric acid solution. Shake briskly, then
strain into a highball glass. Top with sparkling wine
and garnish with edible flowers and Firestix, on a mini
clothespin, if desired.

. . . .

JASMINE TEA GIN
MAKES 750 ML

1 (750 mL) bottle Fords gin

1 tablespoon loose jasmine
tea leaves, preferably
Harney & Sons

Pour the gin into a pitcher or other large container.
Add the loose tea and let steep at room temperature for
4 hours. Strain through a fine-mesh sieve and discard
the solids. Store in an airtight container (the original
bottle will work perfectly); it will keep indefinitely.

MARCO POLO SPRITZ

MAKES 1 DRINK

1 ounce Aperol

½ ounce Seville orange–forward amaro, such as Amaro Angeleno, L'Aperitivo Nonino, or Ramazzotti Aperitivo Rosato

2 ounces passion fruit soda, such as Jarritos or OhFresh (see headnote)

2 ounces chilled Prosecco

Bitter orange is a distinctively Mediterranean flavor that is elevated to high art by the Italians and their vast library of amari. This refreshing drink, Daniel Sabo's ode to citrusy bitterness, allows for some flexibility in the ingredients, provided the amaro chosen has dominant Seville bitter orange flavors. Passion fruit soda can be found in most supermarkets, but in a pinch, LaCroix passion fruit–flavored sparkling water will also work.

In a large wine glass filled with ice, combine all the ingredients and stir once to combine.

MATERIAL GIRL

MAKES 1 DRINK

1 ounce fresh watermelon juice

½ ounce fresh cantaloupe juice

¾ ounce Avión silver tequila

¼ ounce Luxardo Bitter Bianco liqueur

¾ ounce Ramazzotti Aperitivo Rosato

¼ ounce vanilla syrup (see page 170)

¼ ounce citric acid solution (see page 171)

Pinch of kosher salt

Chilled Rene Geoffroy NV Champagne, to top

Watermelon rind, for garnish

Swathed in a captivating pretty pale blush color, Matt Reysen's Material Girl offers more than meets the eye. Perfectly balanced between sweet and bitter, the fresh juices contribute a snap of freshness, which amplifies the Italian liqueurs' nuanced dry notes.

In a highball glass filled with ice, combine the watermelon juice, cantaloupe juice, tequila, Luxardo, Ramazzotti, vanilla syrup, citric acid solution, and salt. Top with Champagne and stir once to combine. Garnish with the watermelon rind.

POCKETFUL OF SUNSHINE

MAKES 1 DRINK

1 ounce Strawberry Cordial (recipe follows)

¾ ounce limoncello, homemade (see page 163) or store-bought

½ ounce chilled Fentimans rose lemonade or similar French-style rose lemonade

1 ounce chilled Veuve Clicquot Rosé Champagne

Lemon twist, for garnish

With its fetching pink blush, subtle berry accents, and not-too-sweet palate, a sip of this drink feels like carrying around a pocketful of sunshine. It's cheerful, designed to please many, and winsomely pretty to behold. If serving this at an event, make the Strawberry Cordial (and the limoncello, if you're not using a store-bought bottle) one day ahead; on the day of the party, just pour into glasses and top with the sparkling rose lemonade and wine.

In a mixing glass filled with ice, combine the strawberry cordial and limoncello. Stir to combine. Strain into a chilled Nick-and-Nora glass. Top with the rose lemonade and Champagne. Garnish with the lemon twist.

STRAWBERRY CORDIAL

MAKES ABOUT 2 CUPS

2 cups hulled and quartered
strawberries

½ cup sugar

¼ teaspoon citric acid

This cordial, a version of which appeared as
Strawberry Consommé in my first book on alcohol-
free cocktails, has been updated here with smaller
portions and a dash of citric acid to extend its shelf life.
As with the original, this cordial captures that farm-
fresh strawberry flavor with little effort, making it a
worthwhile companion for cocktails.

The blanched
strawberries, though
stripped of their color,
are still edible. Rather
than discarding them,
use them in a smoothie
within 1 day.

In a medium saucepan, combine the strawberries and
2 cups water and bring to a simmer over low heat,
about 5 minutes. Remove from the heat, cover, and let
steep until the fruit is pale and the water is bright red,
about 30 minutes. Strain through chef's linen, a fine-
mesh sieve, or a nut-milk bag (see Note). Add the sugar
and citric acid and stir until fully dissolved. Transfer to
an airtight container and let cool completely. Cover and
store in the refrigerator for up to 1 week.

SELLING SUNSETS

MAKES 1 DRINK

1 ounce soju

½ ounce fresh lime juice

½ ounce cane syrup (see page 168)

¼ ounce Giffard Banane du Brésil liqueur

1 teaspoon John D. Taylor's Velvet Falernum

Chilled Champagne, to top

Lime wheel, for garnish

Nutmeg, for grating

Citrusy and vibrantly fresh, Samantha Casuga's Selling Sunsets is a great companion to outdoor cookouts and pool parties. This drink puts a spotlight on lime's beguiling acidity, balancing it against the caramelized sugar and spice undertones of the cane syrup and liqueurs. Fresh lime juice is notoriously fickle and short-lived, with a shelf life of 4 to 12 hours. Juice the limes just before using, or just before guests arrive, if you're serving this at a party. Never use bottled lime juice (see page 8).

In a cocktail shaker with 1 ice cube (see Note), combine the soju, lime juice, cane syrup, banana liqueur, and falernum. Whip shake briskly until the ice is fully broken up. Strain into a highball glass filled with ice and top with Champagne. Garnish with the lime wheel and grate a sprinkling of nutmeg over the top.

NOTE

This drink calls for a whip shake. Add just a small amount of ice (either smaller ice pellets or 1 medium cube) to the tin. Less ice means more air, resulting in a frothy drink. Unlike a traditional shake, you will likely end up with no ice in the tin after whip shaking.

SEVILLE SPRITZ

MAKES 1 DRINK

1 ounce Tanqueray Sevilla Orange gin

½ ounce Pierre Ferrand dry curaçao

1½ ounces chilled orange wine

2 dashes orange bitters

1 drop orange blossom water

½ ounce vanilla syrup (see page 170)

3 ounces chilled Prosecco

Blood orange wheel, for garnish

Orange twist, for garnish

As light and airy as summer linen, the Seville Spritz is a bouquet of gentle orange and vanilla notes, lifted by a light trail of transparent bubbles. Designed by the world-class bar team at New York's Dante, this spritz is dry and refreshing, opening with a soft perfume of orange blossom and closing out with a mineral finish.

In a mixing tin filled with ice, combine the gin, curacao, orange wine, bitters, orange blossom water, and vanilla syrup. Shake to combine, then strain into a highball glass filled with ice. Top with the Prosecco. Garnish with the blood orange wheel and orange twist.

SILK ROAD

MAKES 1 DRINK

½ ounce Fords gin

1½ ounces pear puree

1 ounce Gunpowder-Ginger
Syrup (recipe follows)

4 ounces chilled Cava or
similar sparkling wine

Thin slices of pear, for
garnish

Shaved green cardamom,
for garnish

Gunpowder green tea is a specific style of tea that
has more caffeine than other green teas as well as
a lush, grassy minerality. When paired with fresh
ginger's spiky heat and the yielding sweetness
of pears, the tea unearths sparkling wine's drier
tendencies, calling to mind the chalky terroir, which
can sometimes be buried in cocktails. Refreshing and
unexpected, Daniel Sabo's Silk Road swerves into
savory, dry, and very memorable territory.

In a mixing tin, combine the gin, pear puree, and syrup.
Add ice and shake until cold. Strain into a flute, then
top with the Cava. Garnish with a pear fan (several
thin slices joined by a skewer and arranged like a fan)
and shaved green cardamom.

GUNPOWDER-GINGER SYRUP

MAKES ABOUT 10 OUNCES

1 teaspoon (4 g) loose
gunpowder green tea

6 ounces hot water (optimal
temperature for green tea is
170° to 180°F)

1 cup superfine sugar

2 ounces fresh ginger juice

In a nonreactive container, combine the green tea
and hot water. Steep for 6 minutes. Strain the tea and
discard the solids, then add the sugar and ginger juice.
Stir until the sugar has dissolved and the mixture is fully
combined. Let cool completely, then store in an airtight
container in the refrigerator for up to 1 week.

SOUTHERN BELLE

MAKES 1 DRINK

2 ounces English Breakfast–
Infused Vodka (recipe
follows)

1 ounce fresh lemon juice

½ ounce simple syrup
(see page 168)

10 fresh mint leaves, plus
additional sprigs for garnish

2 ounces chilled
sparkling wine

Lemon wheel, for garnish

Infusing a spirit with tea is a time-tested way to craft an original flavor at home. Daniel Sabo's English breakfast–infused vodka will add savory flair to espresso martinis, traditional fifty-fifty martinis, and even jazz up a vodka-soda. This aptly named recipe evokes languid nights, fluttering fans, and chilled lemonades. All that's missing is a crisp seersucker-and-linen outfit.

In a mixing glass filled with ice, combine the vodka, lemon juice, simple syrup, and mint leaves. Shake briskly to break up the mint. Strain into a highball glass filled with ice, then top with the sparkling wine. Garnish with the lemon wheel and a handful of mint sprigs (also known as a mint crown).

ENGLISH BREAKFAST–INFUSED VODKA
MAKES 1 LITER

1 (1 L) bottle premium vodka

About 3 tablespoons (8 g)
loose English breakfast tea
leaves

In a large container with a lid, combine the vodka and tea and let steep for 24 to 48 hours. Strain the vodka and discard the solids. Store in a nonreactive airtight container at room temperature; it will keep indefinitely.

RHUBARB & STRAWBERRY
HIGHBALL

MAKES 1 DRINK

1 ounce Grey Goose
Essences Strawberry &
Lemongrass vodka

½ ounce Aperol

¾ ounce Briottet Rhubarb
or Giffard Rhubarbe liqueur

Chilled 2022 Nature's
Revenge pét-nat rosé

Pickled Rhubarb (recipe
follows), for garnish

As with fashion and cinema, a French cocktail always stands apart from its peers. Often, a French drink is minimalist yet impeccably composed and frequently features one unexpected detail that turns heads. This is the case with Grey Goose ambassador Maxime Belfand's Rhubarb & Strawberry Highball, which perfectly balances strawberry's sweetness, lemongrass's earthiness, and Aperol's bitter zing. The pickled rhubarb garnish ties the drink experience together with a savory snap that elongates the finish with an intriguing je ne sais quoi.

In a highball glass, combine the vodka, Aperol, and rhubarb liqueur. Add ice, stir once, then top with the rosé. Garnish with the pickled rhubarb.

PICKLED RHUBARB

MAKES ABOUT 2 CUPS

1 cup white wine vinegar

1 cup sugar

2 bay leaves

½ teaspoon whole black peppercorns

1½ teaspoons sea salt

1 teaspoon minced fresh ginger

1 sprig thyme

Zest of ½ small orange

2 tablespoons red pepper flakes

1 pound fresh rhubarb stalks, thinly sliced (about 4 cups)

In a stainless-steel or other nonreactive pot, combine 1 cup water and the vinegar. Add the sugar, bay leaves, peppercorns, salt, ginger, thyme, orange zest, and red pepper flakes. Bring to a boil over medium heat, then reduce the heat to maintain a low simmer and cook, until the sugar has dissolved, about 5 minutes. Remove from heat and let cool, then strain the cooled pickling liquid to remove the larger solids (leave any red pepper flakes that sneak through in the liquid).

Place the rhubarb in a glass or plastic ½-quart jar. Pour the pickling liquid over the rhubarb, making sure it is fully submerged. Cover the container and refrigerate for at least 1 day before using. Store in the refrigerator for up to 1 month. The red pepper flakes will make the mixture spicier over time; if the mix is not spicy enough, add more red pepper flakes.

SUNDAY JULEP

MAKES 1 DRINK

1 ounce Angel's Envy or similar premium bourbon

¾ ounce St. George spiced pear liqueur

¼ ounce vanilla syrup (see page 170)

Crushed ice

2 ounces chilled sparkling wine, to top

Handful of mint sprigs, for garnish

Confectioners' sugar, for garnish

The julep, a Southern staple dating from the 1800s, is traditionally made with brandy or whiskey, fresh mint, and confectioners' sugar. Here the classic recipe gets an update with a full-bodied premium bourbon, a dash of St. George's ambrosial spiced pear spirit, and a splash of crisp, acidic bubbles. Warm vanilla swirls in the glass and in each sip, before sinking into a finish scented with caramelized baking spices.

In a wine glass, combine the bourbon, pear liqueur, and syrup. Stir to combine, then fill to the top with crushed ice. Pour the sparkling wine over the ice, then garnish with the mint and a dusting of confectioners' sugar.

SUNNY DAYS

MAKES 1 DRINK

1½ ounces The Glenlivet 12-year-old Scotch

¾ ounce fresh lemon juice

¾ ounce Turmeric-Honey Syrup (recipe follows)

2 ounces chilled G.H. Mumm Grand Cordon Rosé Champagne

Long orange twist, for garnish

Raspberry, skewered, for garnish

Whiskey, whipped up with fresh lemon and honey syrup? Cocktail fans will recognize the influence of the classic Gold Rush recipe, made famous by the late Sasha Petraske, in the Sunny Days, a sparkling drink created by Pernod Ricard's Jane Danger. In her riff, Jane melds a hearty Scotch and a savory turmeric syrup with Mumm's Grand Cordon Rosé Champagne, which introduces an unexpected floral counterbalance.

In a mixing tin filled with ice, combine the Scotch, lemon juice, and turmeric-honey syrup. Shake briskly to combine, then strain into a wine glass. Top with the Champagne. Garnish with the orange and raspberry skewer.

TURMERIC-HONEY SYRUP

MAKES ABOUT 1¼ CUPS

1 cup boiling water

½ cup honey

1 tablespoon ground turmeric

In a container, stir together the boiling water, honey, and turmeric until well combined. Transfer to a bottle or airtight container and refrigerate; it will keep for up to 2 weeks.

THE SWAN SONG

MAKES 1 DRINK

½ ounce contemporary-style gin, preferably Hendrick's

½ ounce Green Chartreuse

½ ounce Luxardo Maraschino Originale liqueur

½ ounce Italicus Rosolio di Bergamotto liqueur

½ ounce fresh lime juice

1 ounce chilled sparkling wine, to top

Brandied cherry, for garnish (optional)

The Last Word is a beloved Prohibition-era holdover, rediscovered in the craft cocktail era and currently enjoying a long second life as the sophisticate's choice for a sip full of mood and nuance. The original recipe (gin, Green Chartreuse, Luxardo Maraschino, and lime juice in equal ¾-ounce parts) is updated here. The portions here are reduced to make room for a splash of crisp effervescence. Italicus, a bergamot liqueur, balances out the wine's acidity with a soft citrus base that complements, not competes with, Chartreuse's famed herbal accents.

In a mixing tin filled with ice, combine the gin, Chartreuse, Luxardo, Italicus, and lime juice. Shake well to combine, then strain into a coupe. Top with the sparkling wine. Garnish with a brandied cherry, if desired.

THE BRAVOLEBRITY

MAKES 1 DRINK

1½ ounces mezcal, preferably Del Maguey Vida Clásico or El Silencio Espadín

1 ounce Cucumber Lime Cordial (recipe follows)

¼ ounce fresh lime juice

1 ounce sparkling gentian soda, preferably Top Note Gentiana

1 ounce chilled brut sparkling wine

Cured cucumber slices (from Cucumber Lime Cordial; recipe follows) or mini-cucumber slice, for garnish (optional)

Lime wedge, for garnish (optional)

Smoky and unapologetically bitter, think of this drink as a distilled version of an iconic Real Housewife: full of biting acidic asides and a scorched-earth finish that will live rent-free in your head.

The Cucumber Lime Cordial introduces a strident herbaceousness that flirts with mezcal's smoldering charm. Gentian sodas, long popular in Europe, are finally making their way stateside, with American producers, such as Milwaukee's Top Note, releasing their own small-batch tonic made with alpine gentian root. A compellingly bitter snap, as any reality star will tell you, is key to the drink's lasting impression.

In a mixing tin filled with ice, combine the mezcal, cucumber lime cordial, and lime juice. Shake briskly until the ice is broken up. Open the tin and add the gentian soda and sparkling wine. Swirl gently to combine, then strain into a highball glass filled with ice.

Garnish with 1 or 2 cured cucumber slices and the lime wedge, speared on a cocktail pick, or a mini-cucumber slice, if desired.

CUCUMBER LIME CORDIAL

MAKES ABOUT 20 OUNCES

6 small cucumbers, thinly sliced

2 cups thinly sliced celery (with leaves)

Peel of 3 limes

2 cups sugar

½ teaspoon citric acid

2 cups boiling water

In a wide baking dish, combine the cucumber, celery, and lime peels. Add the sugar and citric acid, then toss lightly to combine. Set aside to infuse at room temperature for at least 2 hours or up to overnight; the sugar will slowly melt the oils in the fruit.

Strain the syrup through a conical sieve into a clean container; before discarding the solids, pick out small slices of cucumber and reserve in an airtight container in the refrigerator for 2 to 4 days to use as a garnish. Add the boiling water to the syrup and stir until any remaining sugar has fully dissolved. Strain once more through chef's linen, a super-fine-mesh sieve, or a nut-milk bag to remove any fine particles. Store the cordial in an airtight container in the refrigerator for 3 to 4 weeks.

PASSIFLORA SPRITZ

MAKES 1 DRINK

2 ounces Muscadet, chilled

¾ ounce Salers gentian
aperitif

½ ounce Chinola passion
fruit liqueur

1 teaspoon simple syrup
(see page 168)

Chilled sparkling wine, to top

3 lemon wheels, for garnish

Passiflora is the genus for the passion flower, which
describes over five hundred flowering plants. Natasha
David's Passiflora Spritz is a lilting, floral spritz that
charmingly harmonizes gentian's strident vegetal
tones with passion fruit's candied, zesty notes. Salers
is the oldest producer of gentian liqueurs, classic
French aperitifs similar to Italy's amari, while Chinola
is a relatively new upstart whose passion fruit liqueur
is making cameo appearances on menus in the
world's best bars.

In a wine glass filled with ice, combine the Muscadet,
Salers, Chinola, and simple syrup. Stir well to combine.
Top with sparkling wine. Garnish with the lemon wheels.

VAPORETTO

MAKES 1 DRINK

½ ounce Aperitivo
Cappelletti

¼ ounce fresh lemon juice

Pétillant naturel wine
(see headnote), to top

Castelvetrano olive,
for garnish

Georgette Moger-Petraske is one of Manhattan's foremost hostesses, running intimate Parisian-style salons out of her chic Midtown apartment. Her Regarding Oysters salon is a coveted invitation among the city's elite, offering a night of conviviality, refined manners, and excellent drinks.

The Vaporetto was designed as a welcome cocktail for her Valentine's Sweetheart Salon series and came about as an accident of sorts. "Thinking how lovely the salty-oily-briny elements of a Castelvetrano olive would complement the earthy elements of an Italian pét-nat, I dropped one into my glass," Georgette says. "To my delight, the olive whizzed about like a little motorboat. We turned the concept into a perfect low-ABV cocktail with the addition of Cappelletti and a scant squeeze of lemon for brightness." Georgette advises that any pét-nat will do, but the more natural the better; just avoid any overly sweet sparkling wines.

In a cocktail shaker filled with ice, combine the Cappelletti and lemon juice and briefly stir. Strain into a chilled red wine glass and top with pét-nat. Float the olive in the glass.

LARGE FORMAT

CANDIED PINEAPPLE PUNCH

MAKES 10 TO 15 DRINKS

1 pineapple

½ cup cane sugar or Demerara sugar

Freshly grated nutmeg

4 ounces Plantation Stiggins Fancy Pineapple Rum

4 ounces Hardy Legend 1863 Cognac or similar premium Cognac

4 ounces Grand Marnier

4 ounces fresh lemon juice (from 1 medium lemon)

1 bottle chilled Veuve Clicquot Yellow Label Champagne or similar sparkling wine

The world's first cocktail recipe book—*Jerry Thomas' Bartenders' Guide*—was published in 1862, yet it endures as a source of inspiration for bartenders everywhere. No cocktail book is complete without at least one adaptation from Thomas's cocktail bible.

The original recipe for Pineapple Punch calls for *four* (!) bottles of Champagne or sparkling wine. In this adaptation, I reduced the portions but also chose contemporary ingredients that reference each other: Plantation's pineapple rum is an obvious partner to the fresh pineapple, while Grand Marnier, which is made by macerating oranges in cognac, is a natural choice to pair with Hardy's elegant cognac.

Cut the pineapple in half. Carefully slice off the rind from one half, then thinly slice. In a container, combine the pineapple slices with the sugar. Cover and let stand, shaking or stirring occasionally to break up the sugar, until the sugar has fully dissolved and the mixture is syrupy and thickened, at least 1 hour.

Meanwhile, slice the remaining pineapple half into small triangles, placing them on a baking sheet. Using a kitchen torch, gently sear the fruit so it caramelizes (lightly sprinkle with sugar and nutmeg, if desired). Set aside to cool.

Add the rum, cognac, Grand Marnier, and lemon juice to the container with the pineapple-sugar mixture and stir well to combine. Transfer the mixture to a large punch bowl. Add ice and stir again. Add the Champagne.

Ladle into punch glasses filled with ice and garnish with the caramelized pineapple and a dusting of freshly grated nutmeg.

GINGER KOMBUCHA MIMOSA

**MAKES ABOUT
15 DRINKS**

3 cups fresh orange juice
(from 9 to 10 medium
oranges)

1 cup ginger kombucha,
such as Health-Ade

2½ cups fresh raspberries

2 cups chilled Chandon
Brut Champagne

Larger ice cubes will
keep the mixture
cold, but not dilute it
too quickly. Ice pop
molds or small plastic
containers make great
large ice blocks.

A welcome addition to any gathering, this large-format
four-ingredient drink is a recipe you can put in your
back pocket for all manner of occasions. Depending on
the size of the pitcher you use, you will likely have chilled
wine left over; keep it on ice on the side to top off the
batch (or drinks) as needed.

In a pitcher filled with large ice cubes (see Note),
combine the orange juice and kombucha. Add a
handful of raspberries, reserving the rest for garnish.
Add the Champagne to the mix, reserving the bottle
for topping off. Stir once to combine. Serve in flutes
garnished with raspberries.

CLARIFIED PORN STAR MARTINI

MAKES 1 DRINK

2 ounces chilled Clarified
Porn Star Milk Punch
(recipe follows)

4 ounces chilled Rene
Geoffrey NV Champagne

Passion fruit quarter,
for garnish

There is no ice added,
so the ingredients
should be well chilled
ahead of time.

Clarified milk punches are one of the oldest mixology styles, dating back to the late 1600s, an era before refrigeration. The technique is very simple: Infuse milk with a drink's ingredients, introduce fresh citrus to separate the milk, and then strain away the solids. The result: transparent cocktails with a creamy mouthfeel and a long shelf life. (No, these punches do not taste like milk.) In recent years, this vintage technique has made a comeback at trendy bars. The beverage director of New York's Discolo bar, Matt Reysen, applies the milk punch technique to the classic Porn Star Martini (see page 28), achieving a neat trick the original couldn't: meld into a perfectly translucent cocktail.

This is an aspirational recipe that requires a large volume of ingredients, an investment of time and patience, and the right equipment to clarify properly. That said, the payoff is *worth it.* This is a large-format batch that transforms into a simple two-ingredient pour. Once the milk punch is clarified, it will keep indefinitely in the refrigerator, making it ideal for planned and impromptu celebrations.

Pour the clarified milk punch into a chilled coupe or flute, then top with the Champagne. Garnish with the passion fruit quarter on top of the glass.

CLARIFIED PORN STAR MILK PUNCH

MAKES ABOUT 3 LITERS

42 ounces Absolut vodka

34 ounces whole milk

32 ounces Vanilla Syrup
(see page 170)

8 ounces Dolin Blanc
vermouth

13½ ounces Copalli
white rum

16 ounces fresh lime juice

2½ cups passion fruit puree,
such as Boiron (see Note)

In a large soup pot or other big container, combine all
the ingredients and refrigerate for 24 hours.

Carefully working in small batches, strain the mixture
through a white linen napkin, nut-milk bag, or other
tightly woven material; discard the solids. This first pass
will remove the larger particles; the strained liquid will
resemble cloudy lemonade or unfiltered apple juice.
Strain again using coffee filters; carefully replace filters
as needed. The punch should resemble a white wine, in
that it has a pale honey color, is not cloudy, and is mostly
free of fine particles. (If you want to be extra meticulous,
you can strain the mixture twice through canvas, but
it's not necessary.) Transfer to 1-pint containers and
refrigerate. The punch will keep indefinitely in the fridge.

Boiron is a mainstay at top bars. They make frozen
100% fruit purees, pre-strained and free of seeds,
that are ideal for cocktails. While Boiron purees can
be a bit pricey, they are a worthy investment that saves
time. Find Boiron at culinary mecca Kalustyan's in
New York (order online at https://foodsofnations
.com).

MANDARIN DREAM PUNCH

**SERVES 10 TO 12
(MAKES ABOUT
60 OUNCES)**

2 cups Mandarin Syrup
(recipe follows)

4 cups Psychocandy Tea
(recipe follows)

10 ounces fresh mandarin
juice (from about
8 mandarins)

2 ounces fresh lemon juice
(from 1 medium lemon)

5 ounces Suze herbal
liqueur

2 cups chilled Champagne,
preferably Veuve Clicquot
Brut Yellow Label (half a
bottle)

NOTE

When making this
punch for a party, make
the syrup first so that
the sugar can extract
flavor from the citrus
peels, but don't juice
the fruit until the last
one to two hours before
guests arrive.

The batched drink is a hostess's best friend. A favored
technique of bartenders, batching means combining
all the essential parts of a drink ahead of time and
adding just a finishing touch, or not, before serving.
The benefits of batching include making a drink that's
always consistent and simplifying a recipe procedure
with multiple parts into one simple pour.

Made ahead of time, a batched punch allows you
to serve many drinks at once or can be presented in a
large vessel for guests to serve themselves. This punch,
built to showcase August Uncommon's delightful
Psychocandy tea (a pumpkin-caramel rooibos), is a
fanciful swirl of orange, mandarin, and vanilla flavors.
This is an Orange Creamsicle in drink format, but with
the sophisticated addition of Champagne and a hint of
French botanicals.

In terms of a timeline, steep the tea and, if possible,
the mandarin syrup overnight. Juice the fruits in the
last one to two hours before the festivities begin. Add
the Champagne when guests arrive and you're ready
to serve the punch, or leave it out and add a splash to
individual servings.

In a large serving pitcher or a punch bowl, combine
the mandarin syrup (including the peels), Psychocandy
tea, mandarin juice, lemon juice, and Suze. Stir well
to combine. Add some extra-large ice cubes and stir
briskly again.

Just before serving, pour in the Champagne and stir to
incorporate. (Alternatively, you can serve the punch with
the Champagne alongside, so guests can top their own
cups.) Serve in teacups with 1 large ice cube inside.

MANDARIN SYRUP

MAKES ABOUT 2 CUPS

8 mandarin oranges

1 lemon

2 cups sugar

1 teaspoon citric acid

Peel the mandarins and lemon (reserve the peeled fruit to juice for the punch; submerge the peeled fruits in water until you're ready to use them).

Combine the mandarin and lemon peels, sugar, and citric acid in a 1-quart container. Stir well to combine, then set aside at room temperature to infuse for at least 3 hours before using. (As the mixture rests, the oils in the peels will leech into the sugar and dissolve it, creating a syrup.)

PSYCHOCANDY TEA

MAKES ABOUT 4 CUPS

¼ cup August Uncommon Psychocandy rooibos tea

4 cups boiling water

In a large container, combine the tea and boiling water (or use two 1-quart containers and divide the tea and water evenly between them). Let steep at room temperature overnight. Strain through a fine-mesh strainer into a clean container and discard the solids.

LAMBRUSCO PUNCH

**MAKES 20 TO
25 DRINKS**

17 ounces Fords gin

12½ ounces chilled
sparkling water

8½ ounces fresh lemon juice

8 ounces grenadine

30 dashes Angostura bitters

1 (750 mL) bottle chilled
Lambrusco

2 cups sliced strawberries

Handful of fresh mint, plus
sprigs for garnish

Strawberries and grenadine embellish Lambrusco's
lush fruitiness, while also softening its tannic edges.
Lipstick red, with a fulsome berry-and-mint aroma, this
punch is reminiscent of balmy summer afternoons. The
gin and bitters add savory filters that balance out the
drink's fruitiness.

In a punch bowl or other large container filled with
large ice cubes, combine the gin, sparkling water,
lemon juice, grenadine, and bitters. Stir to combine,
then add the Lambrusco. Add a handful of the
strawberries and mint to the bowl, reserving the
remainder for garnish.

Serve in small rocks glasses or punch glasses filled with
ice, garnished with a strawberry slice and a mint sprig.

STUDIO 75

MAKES 15 TO 20 DRINKS

18 ounces Fords gin

9 ounces St. George spiced pear liqueur

9 ounces fresh lemon juice

12 dashes Angostura bitters

1 (750 mL) bottle chilled Veuve Clicquot Brut Yellow Label Champagne

2 pears, thinly sliced

½ cup star anise pods, for garnish

Stridently fresh yet also timeless, the Studio 75 will be a surefire hit at any party. A pop of bright acidity from the citrus and gin botanicals mellows into a spiced pear perfume buoyed by a chorus of dancing bubbles.

In a pitcher or large container filled with large ice cubes (see Note), combine the gin, pear liqueur, lemon juice, and bitters. Stir to combine, then add the entire bottle of Champagne. Add a handful of pear slices to the mixture, reserving the majority for garnish. Serve the punch in coupes or punch glasses, garnishing each with a pear slice and a star anise pod.

NOTE

If you only have small serving containers, mix the entire batch in a large, heavy soup pot, then transfer to small decorative serving containers, such as glass bottles or pitchers.

THE GROUP TEXT

MAKES 10 TO 12 DRINKS

40 ounces (5 cups) unfiltered apple cider, preferably Zeigler's

8 ounces Irish or American whiskey (see Note)

6 ounces Yuzuri yuzu liqueur

4 ounces Domaine de Canton ginger liqueur

2 ounces fresh lemon juice (from 1 medium lemon)

¼ teaspoon cayenne pepper

1 (750 mL) bottle chilled sparkling wine, to top

Everyone has at least one: a rowdy, chatty, irreverent group text with multiple friends, full of inside jokes, catty comments, and vague plans to meet up IRL. Here's the drink guaranteed to bring the crew together and please everyone.

Full of fan-favorite flavors such as apple, whiskey, lemon, and ginger, this punch comes together easily and is welcome at any hour and any occasion. When I served this at home, the requests for refills outlasted the ingredients.

This drink is made in two parts: The cider-whiskey base, which is built in a container like an iced tea pitcher, is finished with a splash of wine just before serving.

In an iced tea pitcher or similar container, combine the cider, whiskey, yuzu liqueur, ginger liqueur, lemon juice, and cayenne. Add ice, then stir to combine. Chill well.

To serve, pour 3 ounces of the cider-whiskey base into a rocks glass or punch glass filled with ice, then top with 1 ounce of the sparkling wine.

NOTE

The type of whiskey used here is open to preference. Nelson's Green Brier sour mash Tennessee whiskey is my top choice, but bourbon, rye, and Irish whiskey will also shine in this drink.

SNACKS

TATER TOTS
WITH DUCK FAT AND CHILI CRISP

MAKES ABOUT 2 CUPS

½ (32-ounce) bag frozen Ore-Ida tater tots

2 tablespoons rendered duck fat, preferably D'Artagnan, at room temperature

Flaky sea salt

1 tablespoon Asian spicy chili crisp, such as Momofuku Black Truffle Chili Crunch or Lao Gan Ma Spicy Chili Crisp

NOTE

When cooked properly, the tots will flake easily, which can be messy if you're serving them as finger food. If you're hosting a large group, spear each tot with a toothpick, or portion and serve in individual ramekins.

I can't recall when the combination of potatoes and duck fat first entered my consciousness, but some late night in New York City, I nibbled on duck fat–soaked french fries and have never been the same. Duck fat lends crispy potatoes a roundness of flavor that bounces off the salt sprinkles.

Here plump tater tots are tossed in duck fat, then set against the multilayered flavor bomb of a traditional Asian chili crisp. For a vegetarian option, a fragrant olive oil or a rich European butter, such as Plugrà, can be substituted for the duck fat. This recipe can also be made with frozen french fries in place of the tater tots.

Preheat the oven to 450°F.

Arrange the tater tots in a single layer in a deep baking dish. Add the duck fat and toss to fully coat, then bake according to the package instructions, 20 to 25 minutes, or until golden brown. Remove from the oven and let cool slightly. Sprinkle with a pinch of salt.

Arrange the tots in a serving dish (or several—see Note). Serve the chili crisp in a separate small bowl or ramekin alongside the tots.

TRUFFLE BUTTER POPCORN

MAKES 2½ CUPS

2½ cups unsalted plain popcorn

1 tablespoon black truffle butter, melted

Pinch of flaky black sea salt, preferably Big Sur Salts Black Cone Salt

Pinch of coarsely ground black pepper

Is there a more fitting sidekick to sparkling wine than truffles? Their earthy, savory, decadently umami notes provide a perfect backdrop for the crisp acidity of a well-constructed sparkling wine. Consider the timeless pairing of truffle pasta and a well-chilled blanc de blancs. This hostess-friendly snack comes together in mere minutes and can be served for parties of any size or enjoyed as an end-of-the-week solo treat.

Consider this recipe a guideline, which can easily be scaled up for groups. Popcorn takes just minutes to make from scratch, but store-bought popcorn is also great (provided it is unsalted, with no additional flavoring). A great salt can do a lot of lifting here, so indulge in a high-quality flaky sea salt, such as Black Cone Salt by California's Big Sur Salts.

Put the popcorn in a large container with a lid, then pour the melted butter over the top. Sprinkle with the salt and pepper. Cover and shake vigorously to mix (alternatively, mix well with a wooden spoon).

Transfer the popcorn to a serving dish and serve warm or at room temperature.

CHEESE BOARD

Cheese with a higher fat content tends to pair well with sparkling wine, according to Los Angeles–based cheesemonger Jason Velasquez. That's because the bubbles in wine lift the fat molecules on the palate, allowing the layers of flavor in the cheese to unfurl. Jason, who creates cheese boards and savory gift baskets for Hollywood A-listers, notes that two cow's-milk cheeses from the Champagne-Ardenne region of France are great starting points. Langres is densely creamy and is built in molds designed to hold a splash of bubbles, while Chaource has buttery, tangy notes and 50% butterfat, making it ideal to pair with sparkling wines.

Here are some tips for an easy and successful cheese board:

- Assuming there's other food to be had, serve at least ⅓ pound cheese per 4 people.

- Pull the cheese from the fridge at least 30 minutes and up to 1 hour before serving to let it come to room temperature.

- When picking cheeses, an easy guideline is to feature one of each texture: one soft, one semisoft, and one hard. Another option is to pick one from each animal: cow, sheep, and goat.

- Jason suggests getting at least one crowd-pleasing cheese (such as a sharp aged cheddar or a peppery Manchego), then adding something a little more adventurous, such as Persillé de Rambouillet (an ash-covered blue goat cheese) or a decadent truffled Brie.

- Always chat with the cheesemonger at your local cheese shop; they will know what's best and ripest in house.

Given that there are literally hundreds of cheeses to choose from, Jason offers these categories as a general guideline to mix and match from:

- double crème and triple crème
- fromage blanc
- fresh goat
- bloomy rind
- washed rind
- sweet & creamy blue
- buttery
- mildly pungent

Keep the sides simple with one or two dried fruits (such as apricots) and one or two fresh fruits (such as grapes or pears). He adds one jam or honey, noting that honey is a must if a blue cheese is featured (Mike's Hot Honey is an incomparable option). Include one vinegary or pickled element, in the form of cornichons, olives, or capers. Lastly, finish with some crunch or salt, whether in the form of roasted nuts, Corn Nuts, or crisps.

If you include meats, stick to fatty and slightly salty varieties such as dry coppa, jamón Ibérico, or a Prosciutto di Parma. Duck mousse, chicken liver pâté, and foie gras are also classics; pair them with a grainy mustard or a sweet jam (such as cherry or fig). "While it's tempting to load up on accouterments, the cheese is the focus," Jason says. "Give most of the space on the board to the cheese."

ROASTED NUT MIX

MAKES 1⅔ CUPS

⅓ cup raw unsalted hazelnuts

⅓ cup raw unsalted almonds

⅓ cup raw unsalted cashews

⅓ cup raw unsalted pumpkin seeds

⅓ cup raw unsalted sunflower seeds

2 tablespoons unsalted butter, melted

1 tablespoon minced fresh rosemary

1 tablespoon Mike's Hot Honey

½ teaspoon kosher salt

Zest of 1 medium orange

Pinch of flaky sea salt, to taste

Pinch of brown sugar

Inspired by Los Angeles cheesemonger Jason Velasquez's personal recipe, this savory-salty-sweet treat comes together in just a few minutes and is easily customizable to use your favorite nut combinations or whatever you have in the pantry. If you can't find hot honey, substitute maple syrup and a dash of cayenne pepper, or leave the heat out altogether. Look for a mix of textures and sizes in the nuts. Flaky, artisanal salt and a sprinkle of brown sugar finish the mix with a bright, piquant note.

Preheat the oven to 350°F.

In a medium bowl, combine the hazelnuts, almonds, cashews, pumpkin seeds, sunflower seeds, melted butter, rosemary, hot honey, salt, and orange zest and stir until the nuts and seeds are fully coated with butter and honey. Spread the mixture over a shallow baking dish or baking sheet and toast in the oven for 10 minutes. Remove from the oven, stir to ensure everything toasts evenly, and return to the oven for 8 minutes more, until fully toasted. Remove from the oven.

While the nuts are still warm, sprinkle with the flaky salt and brown sugar and stir, then set aside to cool completely before serving or storing. The roasted nuts will keep in an airtight container at room temperature for about 2 weeks or in the refrigerator for about 1 month.

HIGH & LOW
POTATO CHIPS & DIP

Potato chip dip, but grown-up. The classic party dish gets a cheeky upgrade that references uptown caviar blinis yet keeps the salty deliciousness down-to-earth. Consider these dip recipes as two sides of the same coin: Each can be served on its own or alongside the other.

In the case of the onion dip, the briny roe brightens the earthy onion for a satisfying umami mouthful. The roe gives the dip an eye-catching splash of pink that will have people crossing the room for a taste. You can find lovely high-quality small-batch prepared onion dips at specialty stores, including Whole Foods.

Caviar and crème fraîche have long been paired with blinis. In the second dip, caviar is swirled directly into the cream, with an extra dollop on top for the visual flair. Mixing some caviar into the cream means that everyone gets a chance to enjoy the delicacy. (Every hostess knows there's always one guest who tries to take too much caviar.) I also like to mix a little herbed chèvre (a soft, creamy French goat cheese) into the crème fraîche for a touch of piquant spice, but this can be left out, especially if you're already serving the onion dip.

Experiment with a range of potato chip styles and brands, but stick with salted plain (versus flavored) options to let the ocean-salty dip shine brightest.

POTATO CHIPS WITH CAVIAR AND CRÈME FRAÎCHE DIP

MAKES ½ CUP

½ cup crème fraîche, at room temperature

2 ounces chilled caviar

Potato chips, for serving

In a small bowl, combine the crème fraîche and 1 ounce of the caviar. Stir to combine, then dollop the remaining caviar on top. Serve with potato chips on the side.

POTATO CHIPS WITH ONION DIP AND SALMON ROE

MAKES 1 CUP

1 cup onion dip

2 tablespoons salmon roe

Potato chips, for serving

Bring the onion dip to room temperature (ideally, let it sit for about half an hour), then transfer to a small serving dish. Top with the salmon roe. Serve with potato chips on the side.

NOTE

The serving size is flexible for parties. Put out a little at a time so that the roe doesn't get too warm.

CACIO E PEPE DIP

MAKES ABOUT ⅔ CUP

¼ cup extra-virgin olive oil

⅔ cup grated Pecorino Romano cheese

1 teaspoon coarsely ground black pepper

Salted crackers, for serving

Cacio e pepe, the wildly popular Roman dish made with cheese, pepper, and pasta, captured the collective imagination in recent years, with everyone from trained chefs to home cooks making their own variations. What if those rich umami flavors were translated into a dip that comes together in minutes? As satisfying for a group as for solo dinners with a crisp glass of bubbles, this dip can be a component to a cheese board or stand alone with a handful of salted crackers.

In a small saucepan, gently warm the olive oil over low heat for 2 minutes. Remove from the heat. Add the cheese and pepper and mash with a fork until the oil has been fully absorbed. The dip will resemble a thick paste.

Transfer the dip to a small ramekin and serve warm or at room temperature, with salted crackers alongside. If not serving within 2 hours, cover and refrigerate for up to 1 week. Bring to room temperature before serving.

NOTE

The cheese is salty on its own, so resist the urge to add salt (especially since this dip will be served with crackers that likely have salt sprinkles).

Have leftover dip? Mix a spoonful or two of this paste into warm pasta sauce for an instant flavor upgrade.

SARDINES & SEA SALT
CRACKERS

**MAKES ABOUT
24 CRACKERS**

2 tablespoons Trader Joe's garlic aioli mustard sauce or other fine-grain mustard

1 (4.4-ounce) package The Fine Cheese Co. lemon, sea salt, and olive oil crackers or similar

1 (4.2-ounce) package Bar Harbor Wild Petite Sardines in extra-virgin olive oil or similar

½ cup pickled red onion

This delicate snack packs an umami punch that belies its miniature size. Use chef's tweezers or a small fork to handle the sardines, as they break easily. When shopping, opt for skin-on fish in oil over fish packed in water. (Save the oil for salad dressings or pastas.) Also, seek out petite sardines, which are a manageable size for party finger food.

When choosing crackers, look for sturdy artisanal crackers that will hold up under the oil yet won't overwhelm the sardine's signature smokiness. The Fine Cheese Co., a British cracker company, makes many exceptional snacks; their lemon, sea salt, and olive oil crackers are all but the perfect complement for the sardines' oily brininess.

Working carefully, swipe a very thin layer of mustard sauce on each cracker. Top with a petite sardine and 1 or 2 small ribbons of pickled onion. (You may have to trim the onions if they are too large to fit on the cracker.)

SYRUPS & CORDIALS

LIMONCELLO

**MAKES ABOUT
20 OUNCES**

5 medium lemons

16 ounces vodka

½ cup sugar

Limoncello, a cordial made from fresh lemon peels, is a favored palate-cleanser in Italy and other European countries, where it is served in between courses. Small-batch versions can readily be found at specialty stores, but it's pretty easy to make at home.

Just like any recipe, everyone has their own take on technique and ingredients. Some limoncello recipes call for overproof grain vodkas; I prefer to use vodkas that are drinkable on their own to begin with, giving the limoncello the flexibility to shine in a cocktail or be sipped on its own.

Finely peel or grate the lemons, careful to avoid the white pith; set the peeled fruit aside for another use (see Note).

In a 1-quart container, combine the vodka and lemon peels. Cover and set aside at room temperature to infuse for 24 hours, or up to a week for a stronger flavor.

Strain into a glass or plastic container with a lid and discard the solids.

In a small container, combine the sugar and ½ cup hot water and stir until the sugar has dissolved. Add the mixture to the strained vodka and stir to combine. Cover and refrigerate or freeze. It will keep indefinitely.

NOTE

Once peeled, the lemons have a short shelf life. Submerge them in water in a 1-quart container and keep refrigerated until you're ready to juice them. They will keep for 1 to 3 days.

CINNAMON SYRUP

**MAKES ABOUT
14 OUNCES**

6 cinnamon sticks

2 cups sugar

1 cup boiling water

In a medium bowl, combine all the ingredients. Stir to dissolve the sugar, then cover and let sit at room temperature overnight. Strain the syrup into an airtight container. Store in the refrigerator for up to 2 weeks.

HONEY SYRUP

MAKES ABOUT 14 OUNCES

1 cup honey

In a small saucepan, combine the honey and 1 cup water. Warm over very low heat, stirring until the honey has dissolved, 1 to 3 minutes. Remove from the heat and set aside to cool.

Pour the cooled syrup into a lidded glass or plastic container and store in the refrigerator for up to 1 month.

RASPBERRY SYRUP

MAKES ABOUT 1¼ CUPS

1 (10-ounce) package frozen raspberries, slightly thawed

1 cup sugar

Pinch of kosher salt

In a small saucepan, combine the raspberries, sugar, salt, and 1 cup water. Gently cook over low heat, stirring occasionally, for 30 to 45 minutes, until the liquid has reduced slightly and thickened. Remove from the heat and let cool.

Strain through a fine-mesh strainer into a 1-quart container (reserve the solids, if desired; see Note). Cover and store in the refrigerator; the syrup will keep for about 1 month.

NOTE

Don't toss that pulp. The strained raspberries are delicious on top of sharp cheese or spread on toast, or consider layering them on a cracker with foie gras for a decadent take on a PB&J. The berries can even be added to smoothies. Store them in an airtight container in the refrigerator and use within 1 week.

SIMPLE SYRUP

**MAKES ABOUT
12 OUNCES**

1 cup boiling water

1 cup sugar (see Note)

In a medium bowl, combine the boiling water and sugar, and stir well until fully dissolved. Let cool to room temperature, then cover and refrigerate. Store in the refrigerator for up to 1 month.

NOTE

To make cane syrup, which adds more flavor and depth, follow this recipe but swap the granulated sugar for cane sugar, which is made from evaporated sugarcane juice.

STRAWBERRY SYRUP

**MAKES ABOUT
1½ CUPS**

1 cup chopped hulled strawberries

1 cup sugar

⅛ teaspoon citric acid

Pinch of kosher salt

In a small saucepan, combine the strawberries, sugar, citric acid, salt, and 1 cup water. Set the pot over very low heat and cook, stirring occasionally, for about 30 minutes (do not let the mixture come to a boil). Once the strawberries are pale and the water is bright red, set aside to cool.

Transfer the strawberry mixture to a high-speed blender or food processor and blend. Strain through a fine-mesh sieve into an airtight container. Store in the refrigerator for up to 2 weeks.

VANILLA SYRUP

**MAKES ABOUT
14 OUNCES**

1 cup boiling water

1½ teaspoons vanilla paste

2 cups sugar

In a medium bowl, combine the boiling water and the vanilla paste and stir well. Add the sugar and stir until the sugar has fully dissolved. Let cool to room temperature, then cover and refrigerate. The syrup is best used within 10 days, but will keep for up to 3 weeks. To extend the life of the syrup, split it up into smaller containers and freeze for up to 1 month.

CITRIC ACID SOLUTION

MAKES 3½ CUPS

2 teaspoons citric acid

A balanced cocktail has elements of sweet as well as sour, but sometimes, bartenders don't want to introduce sour elements through citrus juice. Think of citric acid as the sour counterpart to simple syrup (or as the salt component in culinary recipes); it's there to enhance the flavors of other ingredients but remains in the background. Bartenders will typically use only a few small dashes of citric acid in drinks.

Citric acid is a natural preservative; when added to juices and cordials, it extends their shelf life, especially if they incorporate volatile organics like lime and lemon juice, which have a short window of freshness. A citric acid solution will bring zing to your cocktails, and since the citric acid is a preservative, you can keep the solution in your fridge for months.

In a glass or plastic container, stir together 3½ cups water and the citric acid to combine. Cover and store in the refrigerator for up to 6 months.

ACKNOWLEDGMENTS

Thank you, Team Sparkling.

Eternal gratitude to my agent, Leigh Eisenman, who worked so hard to make this happen, and my editor, Caitlin Leffel, and her team at Union Square & Co., who trusted my vision.

Thank you to my incomparable creative team—Robert Bredvad, Maeve Sheridan, and Mallory Lance. It's a rare gift to connect with people who share the same aesthetics, enthusiasm, and work ethic.

Thank you to the class-act team at LVMH's prestige wines division, specifically the effortlessly charming Sarah Pallack, Nelson Elliott, Katarina Wos, and Anne-Sophie Stock. From coordinating last-minute visits to maisons to sending invitations to interview experts, you have all been crucial to the research and development of this book.

Eternal gratitude to the world-class publicists at LaForce—Ana Rallis, Leslie Pitts, Katie McShan Holmes, Lizzie Stoldt, and the entire prestige wines team. You have been hearing about this project since before it started, and you were helpful until the very end.

Thank you, Bernadette Knight, Anne-Louise Marquis, and the Campari Group. The Sbagliato viral moment was the sparkling cocktail recipe heard around the world, and I don't think any of us will ever (thankfully) recover.

Thank you to the many talented wine and spirits publicists who assisted behind the scenes with introductions, interviews, and recipe sourcing. I can't express how much you were all a lifeline. XOXOs to besties Jenna Kaplan from This One PR for Death & Co and Zacapa rum; Michael Papirmeister from Nike Communications for Bacardi; Kate Kenny from Pernod Ricard; Megan Reeves from Nicolas Feuillatte; Madeleine Andrews from KLG PR; and David Semanoff from Fords Gin.

Thank you, Colin Appiah. Your behind-the-scenes help was truly a godsend, and you represent everything I love about this industry.

Thank you to my beloved best friend Will Davis from Shadow PR. Forever grateful for your friendship, your whip-smart humor, and your willingness to order Dom Pérignon every time we go out.

Thank you to every winemaker, chef de cave, and wine executive I interviewed for this book. Not all the background info made it into the essays, but every conversation was an education.

Massive hug to Jason Velasquez, who is not only a talented cheese resource but also my little brother. I'm very proud to finally be able to work with you.

Lastly, thank you to the bartenders who contributed recipes to this publication. Every contributor is someone I'm proud to call a friend. Not only are these recipes from bartending's top talents, the contributors are an intentionally diverse mix of races, genders, and orientations, representing where mixology is going next.

CONTRIBUTOR BIOGRAPHIES

Douglas Ankrah was the highly lauded Ghana-born British mixologist and entrepreneur who cofounded the London Academy of Bartending (LAB) in 1996 and Townhouse in 2002. Ankrah is credited with inventing the instantly iconic Porn Star Martini in 2005, and launched a ready-to-drink version in 2017.

Maxime Belfand is New York's Grey Goose Ambassador and the former beverage director at AvroKO Hospitality Group and head bartender at Manhattan's Saxon + Parole. His cocktails have been featured in publications such as *Wine Enthusiast*, *Thirsty*, and *Imbibe Magazine* and on Liquor.com.

Tyson Buhler joined the critically acclaimed craft cocktail bar Death & Co in 2012. He later moved into the head bartender position at the famous bar's New York location before becoming Director of Food & Beverage for the company. Tyson was also the 2015 US finalist in the USBG World Class cocktail competition.

Erick Castro is a co-owner of San Diego's lauded Raised by Wolves. An acclaimed beverage director, podcaster, and mentor, Erick was named one of *Drinks International*'s "Bar World 100" most influential industry figures in 2021 and 2023. His beverage programs have earned the highest accolades, including a James Beard Award nomination for Outstanding Bar Program, *Esquire*'s "Best Bars in America," *Food & Wine*'s "World's Best Bars" and multiple Spirited Award nominations at Tales of the Cocktail for "Best American Bartender," "Best Mentor," and "Best Brand Ambassador." In 2019, Erick's *Bartender at Large* podcast won the Tales of the Cocktail Spirited Awards for "Best Broadcast, Podcast or Online Video Series" and "Best Nightclub & Bar Show Industry Podcast of the Year."

Samantha Casuga is the head bartender at the newly reinvented Temple Bar in New York City. A veteran of award-winning cocktail bars (she was previously a head bartender at Dead Rabbit), Samantha has participated in and won numerous bartending competitions, most notably as the New York finalist for the USBG's "Most Imaginative Bartender" award in 2018. Now a judge herself, she also cultivates leadership roles in the drinks community, with roles in committees at San Antonio Cocktail Conference, Tales of the Cocktail, and Bar Convent Brooklyn.

Natasha David's cocktails have been featured in multiple publications, including the *New York Times* and the *Wall Street Journal*, and books, including *Cocktail Codex*, *Nightcap*, and *The Japanese Art of the Cocktail*. A bar industry veteran with stints at Danny Meyer's Maialino, Keith McNally's Pulino's, Maison Premiere, Mayahuel, and Donna, she is the author of *Drink Lightly*. Natasha was named one of Zagat's 2014 "30 Under 30," Eater's 2014 New York and national Bartender of the Year, and StarChef's 2015 Rising Star. In 2020, *Imbibe Magazine* named her Bartender of the Year.

Jane Danger began her bartending career at New York's famed punk rock club CBGB. She later opened a number of Manhattan's iconic bars, including Please Don't Tell, Cienfuegos, and Mother of Pearl, and has produced cocktail programs for international music festivals like Coachella, Bonnaroo, Outside Lands, and Panorama. She is currently the National Mixologist for Pernod Ricard and the author of two books, *Cuban Cocktails* and *The Bourbon Bartender*.

Meaghan Dorman is the creative and hospitality force behind Manhattan's Dear Irving and Raines Law Room, which has three locations across the city. In 2015, Dear Irving was a top ten finalist for "Best New American Cocktail Bar" at Tales of the Cocktail, and was listed in *Esquire*'s 2015 "Best Bars in America." Meaghan was *Imbibe Magazine*'s 2016 Bartender of the Year. In 2022, Dear Irving on Hudson was a Tales of the Cocktail top four finalist for "Best U.S. Hotel Bar" and Meaghan was a top four finalist for "U.S. Bar Mentor."

Marc du Jonchay is a French bartender who trained in New York and is now based in London. Formerly at Discolo and Gage & Tollner, he is now an ambassador with ODVI Armagnac and Banhez Mezcal.

Trevor Easton Langer is a veteran of some of New York's most popular bars, including The Happiest Hour, Slowly Shirley, Employees Only, Dear Irving on Hudson, The Polynesian, and Jac's on Bond.

Brian Evans is the bar director at Sunday Hospitality, which oversees properties including the Chelsea Hotel, Sunday in Brooklyn, El Quijote, and Rule of Thirds.

Earlecia Richelle Gibb is St-Germain's national brand ambassador. In 2020, she was a "Best Brand Ambassador" finalist at Tales of the Cocktail's Spirited Awards and an *Adweek* Experiential Awards finalist for "Experiential Activation by a Spirits Brand."

Ernest Hemingway is one of America's most famous novelists and journalists. The author of numerous titles, including *For Whom the Bell Tolls*, *A Farewell to Arms*, and *The Sun Also Rises*, he was awarded the 1953 Pulitzer Prize for Fiction for *The Old Man and the Sea* and the Nobel Prize for Literature in 1954.

Ben Hopkins cut their teeth behind the bars of Momofuku Ssäm Bar, Momofuku Kō, and Please Don't Tell. They currently serve as the beverage director of HiLot, a disco cocktail bar in Manhattan's Alphabet City.

Aaron Polsky notched over a decade of serving and developing cocktails at premier bars in New York and Los Angeles before becoming an entrepreneur in the ready-to-drink cocktail space with LiveWire, which offers craft cocktail quality drinks created by mixologists. In 2021, *Wine Enthusiast* named Polsky as one of their "40 Under 40 Tastemakers."

Linden Pride is a founding partner of Dante in New York City, which was named the World's Best Bar in 2019 by both World's 50 Best Bars and Tales of the Cocktail. Linden and Dante, with its menu focused on Italian apertivi and cocktails, are credited with contributing to the newfound popularity of Negronis, Sbagliatos, and Garibaldis.

Georgette Moger-Petraske is an acclaimed wine and spirits journalist and the author of the best-selling drinks memoir *Regarding Cocktails*. A consummate hostess, you can find her at Regarding Oysters, the weekly oyster and cocktail salon she runs out of her Midtown apartment.

Brooks Moyer was head bartender at Cool World in Greenpoint, Brooklyn. He previously worked at Endswell and the Van Brunt Stillhouse in Brooklyn, as well as at District in San Francisco.

Maxwell Reis is a bartender and agave aficionado who cultivates relationships with small producers in Mexico, allowing him access to limited-run batches of mezcal that he serves at Hollywood destination bars, including Los Feliz's Mirate, where he is the beverage director.

Matthew Reysen was StarChef's Rising Star in 2023. With a hospitality background that includes head bartender positions at some of New York's most acclaimed bars (Dante, Dead Rabbit, Temple Bar), he took on the role as bar director for Mel's, Discolo, and Michelin-starred Al Coro. He is currently the operations manager for Dante.

Daniel Sabo is a veteran beverage director who has worked for a number of hotels in Los Angeles, including the Ace Hotel DTLA, Palisociety, and the Fairmont Century Plaza. He currently oversees food and beverage operations and hospitality for the Hollywood Roosevelt, which was built by Douglas Fairbanks, Mary Pickford, and Louis B. Mayer, and was the home of the first Academy Awards in 1929.

Alyssa Sartor is an entrepreneur and brand consultant who grew up in the hospitality business, and mines her Italian American heritage for inspiration for her drinks. Alyssa's take on the amaretto sour for her first venue, August Laura, was listed as number one in *Time Out New York*'s "Best Drinks of 2016."

Haera Shin's career has taken her from Hotel 50 Bowery with Chef Dale Talde and John Bush to the Tao Group's Dream Downtown Hotel. She oversees beverage operations for Momofuku, and her signature drinks combine her Korean heritage with a contemporary twist.

Christian "Suzu" Suzuki-Orellana was born into a restaurant industry family, and his drinks are inspired by his grandparents' hospitality as well as flavors and memories of his childhood in Tokyo. He was a competitor on Netflix's *Drink Masters*, a national finalist for the Bacardí Legacy Cocktail Competition in 2018, and a finalist for the USBG's "Most Imaginative Bartender" award in 2020. In 2021, he became one of *Punch*'s Bartenders in Residence, and the following year, he was featured on *Imbibe Magazine*'s "Imbibe 75" list. He was also a top ten finalist for Tales of the Cocktail's "Bartender of the Year" in 2022 and 2023.

David Wondrich is an award-winning drinks historian, author, mixologist, and educator. An English professor who became the longtime drinks correspondent for *Esquire*, Dave has written five cocktail history books, including *Imbibe!*, which was the first cocktail title to win a James Beard Award. He and Noah Rothbaum edited 2022's *Oxford Companion to Spirits & Cocktails*, a compendium of drinks industry knowledge.

Jason Velasquez began his cheese-industry journey as a teenager, when he began working the counter at Silver Lake's Say Cheese. An advocate for refined cheese boards, he currently works at Pasadena's Agnes Cheesery.

ENDNOTES

· · · · · · · · · · · · · · · · · · · ·

WHERE "WINE FLOWED IN RIVERS": Henry Vizetelly, *A History of Champagne: With Notes on the Other Sparkling Wines of France* (1882), 13.

WHICH OCCURRED NATURALLY FOLLOWING A SECONDARY FERMENTATION IN BOTTLES: Tilar J. Mazzeo, *The Widow Clicquot: The Story of a Champagne Empire and the Woman Who Ruled It* (New York: HarperCollins, 2008), xvii–xviii.

THE BRITISH FIRST DISCOVERED HOW TO INDUCE BUBBLES IN WINE: Ibid., xviii.

". . . REQUIRED TO MAKE SPARKLING CHAMPAGNE," MAZZEO REPORTS: Ibid., 32.

80 PERCENT OF ALL THE CHAMPAGNE DRUNK IN AMERICA: *The Journal* (New York, NY), January 5, 1896, p. 17. Retrieved from the Library of Congress, www.loc.gov/item /sn84031792/1896-01-05/ed-1/.

"THE DESIRE TO 'CELEBRATE' IS THE CAUSE OF IT," THE *JOURNAL* REPORTED: "Thirst: New York Has Broken the Champagne Drinking Record This Year by Many Millions of Bottles," *New York Journal*, August 13, 1899.

PREDICTED THE END-OF-YEAR TRENDS FOR 1900: *New York Tribune*, October 24, 1900, p. 7. Retrieved from the Library of Congress, www.loc.gov/item/sn83030214/ 1900-10-24/ed-1/.

INDEX

· · · · · · · · · · · ·

Page references in *italics* refer to photos of recipes.

ABOUT THE AUTHOR

ELVA RAMIREZ is a spirits journalist, video producer, and media strategist who began her career at the *Wall Street Journal*. Her byline has appeared in *Bloomberg Businessweek*, *Rolling Stone*, *Town & Country*, *DuJour*, *Elle*, and *Forbes*. She holds master's degrees from Columbia University and an MBA from Baruch College Zicklin School of Business.